Augusta Evans Wilson

Augusta Evans Wilson
1835-1909

A BIOGRAPHY

by WILLIAM PERRY FIDLER

1951
UNIVERSITY OF ALABAMA PRESS

PRINTED AND BOUND BY THE
BIRMINGHAM PRINTING COMPANY
BIRMINGHAM, ALABAMA

0-8173-5026-8 (pbk: alk. paper)

To

LILY BRAGG and ALICE FIDLER

Preface

I AM INDEBTED to many people for assistance in preparing this biography. To those who cannot be mentioned in this brief space, I express my appreciation again for their helpful suggestions.

My special thanks go to Miss Lily Bragg of Mobile, a niece of Augusta Evans Wilson. With strictest regard for accuracy and intellectual honesty, Miss Bragg answered hundreds of questions, sent clippings and references, and twice read and criticized the manuscript of this book. It is a fortunate biographer who enjoys the kind of assistance which Miss Bragg has rendered.

Miss Mary Gaillard and her father, Mr. S. Palmer Gaillard, also gave valuable aid. They furnished much information about Ashland and the Wilson family, and both read portions of the manuscript.

Mr. Floyd Tillery, whose discriminating judgment has influenced hosts of friends and a score of books, also read and criticized the manuscript.

Mrs. Ruth Evans Dallis of LaGrange, Georgia, and Mrs. Lucile Cary Lowry of Dallas, Texas, supplied me with clippings and many fruitful suggestions. Professor Virginia Peck of Troy, Alabama, obtained microfilms of ten letters and several clippings. Professor Napier Wilt of the University of Chicago gave much helpful advice.

A master's thesis on Mrs. Wilson, submitted to the Alabama Polytechnic Institute by the late Mr. Sidney Phillips of Mobile, was useful in tracing the location of several sources.

I am grateful to the following people, all Alabamians, for assistance in obtaining letters and other biographical data: Mrs. W. B. Paterson, Miss Mabel Heustis, and Mrs. Elizabeth Morris of Mobile; Mrs. Rosalie Heustis Clark, Mr. James E. Rice, and Mr. Frank Trueman of Birmingham; Miss Melissa Wyman and Professor Burke Johnston of Tuscaloosa; Mr. Edward Carothers of Troy; Mr. F. M. Howard of Autaugaville; Miss Annette Howard of Tuskegee; Mrs. R. F. Smith of Oakhill; and Mrs. Edith Crenshaw Tatum of Greenville.

A unique method of research was opened to me by the newsmagazine *Time,* whose editors kindly printed a letter requesting admirers of Mrs. Wilson to send me information on biographical materials. Nearly a hundred answers were received from all parts of this country, and there was one from Australia, one from New Zealand, and another from a naval officer in Zamboanga. A few people in my own neighborhood read the letter in *Time* and supplied useful papers. Encouraged by the cooperation of *Time,* I sought the assistance of Southern newspapers, four of which not only printed my letter but published unsolicited editorials on the subject of my research. These four were the Tuscaloosa *News,* the Mobile *Press Register,* the Columbus (Georgia) *Ledger Enquirer,* and the Birmingham *News.* Another hundred responses came from their readers.

A few of the people mentioned above were among those who answered these published inquiries. Other helpful suggestions came from Dr. E. P. Lipscomb of

Rochester, New York; Mr. W. C. Woodall and Miss Florence Slade of Columbus, Georgia; Dr. Edward H. Cary of Dallas, Texas; Colonel J. M. Prentice of Sydney, Australia; Dr. Eugene S. Sugg of Indianapolis, Indiana; and Mr. Starr Kealhofer, Sr., of Austin, Texas.

Though my debt is great to these generous people, I assume full responsibility for the point of view and the errors of this book.

WILLIAM PERRY FIDLER

University, Alabama
March, 1951

Contents

Illustrations

Augusta Evans Wilson

CHAPTER I: PROLOGUE

Mirror of Victorian Tastes

A HOST OF Victorian readers once believed that Augusta Evans Wilson's influence upon American character and manners was so great that her place in literary history was assured. Critics often attacked her nine romances for their erudite style, their moralizing and excessive pathos, but these qualities seemed to heighten the enthusiasm of her loyal followers, who continued to demand that her books be kept in print. This audience must be considerable even in our time, for her novels are constantly re-issued.

In the author's lifetime her constituents wrote hundreds of letters to her, and many of them made pilgrimages to her elegant home in Mobile, to assure her that *St. Elmo* or *Beulah* or *Macaria* had affected them deeply and they were grateful. Apparently they did not miss the realism which critics insisted was absent in her delineations. What they did find in these romances seemed to please them very much: idealized heroines and heroes, luxurious and exotic mansions and gardens, dignified language, brocaded furnishings, eloquent marriage proposals, and stern punishments for the vicious and hypocritical. Her readers were not trained to expect photographic realism. Their tastes would have made them suspicious of mere observation because they believed that the first duty of art, including fiction, is to elevate—to "do good," as they quaintly put it.

Perhaps the strongest appeal of Mrs. Wilson's books is that of "remembrancer," as one critic wrote.[1] Her novels are like mirrors of a better time, are cherished reminders of social traditions and standards of conduct once honored but often forgotten in a later day. Librarians and booksellers say that this appeal is chiefly responsible for her continued vogue.

Augusta Evans Wilson's private life contrasts with her books in certain ways, for she came into contact with many rowdy and sensational events in our country's expansion westward. As a child in the frontier town of Columbus, Georgia, she saw the militia (of which her father was a member) suppress an insurrection of angry Creek Indians who resented encroachments upon their reservations in eastern Alabama. A little later she was a participant in other stages of American "progress": adaptation of the frontier to the traditions of mansion life, enjoyment of the privileges of a slave-holding society, and escape in a covered wagon from the humiliations of bankruptcy. She had a close-up view of the Mexican War while residing in the remote outpost of San Antonio, and later she wrote a quaint little novel about the famous city.

During the cold war of 1850-1859 Augusta's principal interests were non-political, but in the closing years of the national debate she responded to the challenge of yankee abolitionists with a vigorous and persuasive defense of the South. Unsigned articles were written for newspapers and magazines, and after hostilities began she composed such an effective piece of Confederate propaganda, in her novel *Macaria,* that a Federal general forbade his troops to read it and confiscated available copies. She won a citation from General P. G. T. Beauregard for her services as morale builder and war nurse, and her letters to such influential statesmen as J. L. M. Curry and Benjamin H. Hill prove that her advice in political matters was often sought. Through her activities in support of the South she won the friendship and esteem of such famous Confederates as Toombs, Hilliard and Beauregard, as well as Curry and Hill. At the close of the war she raised funds from among her impoverished friends for the removal of the bodies of fallen Mobilians to Magnolia Cemetery, and later she conducted a drive to finance the erection of a monument to these men. Her zeal for the Confederacy was such that she never used the defeat of her people or the pangs of Reconstruction as subject matter for fiction. To the day of her death she continued to believe that the cause had been sacred.

The height of her reputation came in 1867 with the publication of *St. Elmo,* a success which ranked after *Uncle Tom's Cabin* as the most astonishing American literary bonanza up to that time. A year later she made the kind of brilliant marriage which her virtuous heroines usually attained, becoming mistress of stately Ashland, with its matchless grounds, its liveoaks, greenhouses and camellias which visitors never forgot. Her unique collection of flowering shrubs, ferns and bulbs was better known locally than her books. For fifty years Mrs. Wilson was certainly the first lady of Mobile, probably of Alabama, and visitors in the old city considered an interview with Miss 'Gusta as the leading attraction of the place. Mobilians still revere her memory, and tourists are always directed to the places associated with her life.

Like Benjamin Franklin's private story, hers is American to the core: rise from poverty to mansion luxury, with a strong implication in the heroine's acceptance of events that virtue, attended by circumspection, must inevitably find its just reward.

The stirring intellectual movements of the last century made a deep impression upon her character. Like most of the earnest thinkers of that "Reflective age," as Emerson boastfully described his time, Augusta Evans Wilson fought the battle of Fundamentalism versus Speculation, and she recorded the progress of her assurances step by step in letters and in *Beulah*. She knew her Carlyle, Wordsworth and Emerson so thoroughly that she could cite the texts of German Transcendentalism from which they took their arguments. Her correspondence and her books reflect her prodigious reading and constant thoughtfulness on such diverse movements as the Oxford, the Feminist, the Populist, Evolution, and even Spiritualism.

With respect to some of her views, we may call her *modern*, but this accolade which we self-consciously bestow upon a few Victorians is one that Augusta would not have welcomed without reservations. On most subjects she was a "golden age-ist," a believer in the superiority of the past. She was not so sure, as many of us are today, that tolerance on all points is a virtue. In short, she marched confidently and naturally in the pageant of Victorianism, reflecting its zeal for soul-searching and its love of grandeur, tradition and sentiment.

Mrs. Wilson's peculiar merit as a "domestic sentimentalist"[2] is that her books contain a few attractions which are uncommon in the works of her popular rivals, a group whom Hawthorne once petulantly described as "the damned mob of scribbling women."[3] Even her stilted language, so often condemned and parodied by critics for its affectation, has variety and occasional pungency. She honored the precepts of her age, but she spiced her moralizing with a dash of Byronic gusto. Her best known figure, St. Elmo Murray, is made so fascinating in his sinfulness that "he bowled over a whole generation of romantic schoolgirls." She extended the range of her influence by satisfying her countrymen's hunger for culture, filling her books with commentaries upon philosophy and the arts, upon great writers, musicians and artists. These passages offer refreshment to one who treads his way through this lachrymose fiction which our grandparents read so attentively.

The Victorian tastes which approved these mellow romances need careful analysis, but ridicule is not the proper frame of mind for such criticism. No matter what we may think of these lavendered versions of human nature, the conditions which created them were permeated with sincerity and thoughtfulness, and if we are to understand those times, our mood must be respectful.

Here, then, is the story of a vigorous, zealous woman who mirrored the tastes of the day and influenced her times. Hers was a full life, eventful, helpful and colorful, but her principal achievement was the creation of an odd literary product which millions of our countrymen applauded. Just as ridicule of her books is unsuited to the purposes of this study, so defense of them as works of art is unwise. Rather, let us try to determine why these works happened to satisfy the tastes of people who, in spite of their different fashions and manners, were fundamentally not unlike ourselves.

If these historical perspectives seem inadequate to those who believe that Augusta Evans Wilson's reputation should not be disturbed at this late date, can we not assure these modern folk that another kind of enjoyment may be found in perusing these records? Is it not flattering to see proof of our own superior tastes, to know that we, unlike our forefathers, never mistake an inferior novel for a great one and never allow the pressures of faulty taste around us to confuse our exquisite judgments?

CHAPTER II

Columbus, Georgia

1828-1845

IN THE SPRING of 1828 an English seadog, Captain Basil Hall, journeyed by stagecoach across Georgia to the valley of the Chattahoochee, where he saw a strange but representative example of American pioneering. There on the frontier, in a wilderness acquired only three months before from hesitant Indians, the Captain's party arrived, as he relates, "in the nick of time to see the curious phenomenon of an embryo town—a city as yet without a name, or any existence in law or fact, but crowded with inhabitants, ready to commence their municipal duties at the tap of an auctioneer's hammer." Impressed by this unique method of empire-building, the Englishman recorded every stage of the adventurous enterprise in his *Travels in North America.*[4]

With the "extinction of the Indian claims" and the removal of the last unwilling Creek to reservations across the river in Alabama, the Georgia legislature undertook the plotting of the new city on a site just opposite the old Indian town of Coweta. A few yards upstream were the shelf-like falls, so valuable as sources of water power, and immediately below the falls was the head of the navigable channel which extended to the Gulf. In planning the future city, the surveyors reserved spaces for wide streets, churches, municipal and county buildings, schools and playgrounds. Advertisements of the sale of lots appeared in the principal newspapers throughout the nation, the Captain states, and "sixty days were considered sufficient to enable adventurers, settlers, land speculators, merchants, and all others so disposed, to come to the spot preparatory to the auction." The project "took like wildfire, and the advantages of the new city being loudly proclaimed over the land, people flocked from all quarters to see and judge of it for themselves." Many of them probably came to witness the excitement, but hundreds of future citizens chose the lots for which they would offer bids, and awaited the great day with impatience, bedding themselves in their wagons or in ramshackle huts, cooking their meals over campfires.

When the sale began on the morning of July 10, 1828, over three thousand eager spectators watched the auction.[5] In less than two weeks 488 lots had been sold, the total receipts being $130,991. Nicholas Howard of Greensboro (an uncle of Augusta Evans Wilson) and Peter Dudley bought the choice lot for $1,855, on the corner of Broad and Crawford Streets, and immediately laid plans to construct a hotel to be named after the newly christened town—Columbus. Before the settlement had legal sanction, the Columbus *Enquirer* was established by Mirabeau Bonaparte Lamar, who later became a hero of the Texas War of Independence and second President of the new republic.

The building of Columbus was a project that would have warmed the heart of Mark Twain's Colonel Sellers — a giant undertaking, embellished with the wanderlust and risk and glory of American pioneering. There was one young man among the eager prospectors by the name of Mathew Ryan Evans (called "Matt" throughout his life), a dreamer with much of Colonel Sellers' gentleness, charm and instability. But unlike the whimsical Colonel, Matt Evans had a few years of brilliant success. With his brother, Thomas Crenshaw Evans, he left his father's plantation in Edgefield District, South Carolina, and settled in Columbus within the first two years of the city's founding. The two young brothers established the mercantile firm of M. R. Evans & Company, and Matt began to acquire considerable land from the Indians near Oswitchee in Russell County, Alabama.[6]

As profits rolled in from his store and plantation, Matt Evans was enabled to move in the best society of the booming town. One of his close friends was Colonel Seaborn Jones, a prominent civic leader of Columbus, who was to become a Congressman within a few years. The Colonel's daughter, Mary Jones, married Judge H. L. Benning, for whom the army camp was later named. Another intimate friend was John H. Howard, who had moved from Milledgeville before 1830 and immediately demonstrated his confidence in the frontier town by establishing the first cotton mill along the falls of the Chattahoochee. The first meeting of Matt Evans and Sarah Skrine Howard probably occurred at the graceful estate of John H. Howard, called Wildwood, for Sarah often came over from Baldwin County to visit her brother. Early in 1834 Matt became engaged to the modest and brilliant Sarah.

The prospective marriage of Matt Evans and Sarah Howard linked two old Southern families, both of which had been prominent in the affairs of their country. Eminent branches of the Calhoun and Crenshaw families of South Carolina were related to Matt. John Howard of Milledgeville, Sarah's father, had served in the American Army of the Revolution; her paternal grandfather was Nehemiah Howard, a Revolutionary patriarch who condemned the policies of the British army of occupation in South Carolina so boldly that he was sought out by a delegation of prominent Tories and British officers. According to the family genealogist, Nehemiah met the delegation in front of his plantation home at Cross Keys and was immediately attacked by a British officer with a sword, "who commenced slashing and cutting at [Nehemiah's] head as though determined on severing it from his body. With his walking cane he warded off the blows, until the officer . . . desisted from his dastardly attack, and while no blood was spilled, the hacks upon the walking cane many years after were shown to his sons, which sent a throb to their bosoms of hate to tyranny, which we hope will descend to the latest of his progeny."[7] Nehemiah's most famous descendant, his great granddaughter Augusta Evans Wilson, inherited a large portion of his pluck and zeal.

Though too crippled to fight in the field, Nehemiah Howard advertised his Patriot sympathies—especially his willingness to let his fifteen-year-old son John serve in the Revolutionary Army—and so infuriated the Loyalists and British of Union District that they set fire to his home three times. After years of unpleasant hostility with reactionary neighbors, Nehemiah sold his property at Cross Keys in 1787 and moved to Elbert County, Georgia, near the juncture of the Savannah River and Lightwood Log Creek. His son John, who came out of the army as a major, settled near Milledgeville and was soon a very wealthy planter.

It would seem that these ancestors of Augusta Evans had won fame enough for one American line, but in later years there were cousins of the novelist who sought to identify this branch of the Howards with the noble family in England, whose daughters had married several members of the royal family. All evidence linking Nehemiah with the English noblemen named Howard is merely conjectural. His kinship with the Howards of Virginia and Maryland is more likely, but authentic evidence is also lacking here. The motto in the coat-of-arms of the English Howards, "Sola virtus invicta," might well have been adopted by Nehemiah and his descendants, particularly Augusta Evans; however, when the modest novelist spoke of the "nobility" of her forbears, she had reference only to their pious and charitable virtues.

July 15, 1834, was chosen as the wedding day for Matt and Sarah Evans. The plans of this young couple matched the expansiveness and excitement of flush times around them. They bought 143 acres of wooded land near the estate of Seaborn Jones, and Matt employed an architect to design a house as elegant as the mansions of his bride's relatives. Prominent Georgians who later resided in the Evans house describe the enormous white columns, four feet thick, supporting the massive roof which extended to cover the veranda on the front and two sides. In the interior, all woodwork, except the heart-of-pine floors, was of mahogany—the graceful spiral staircase, the banisters and heavy newel posts, the molding and wainscoting, the massive folding doors, and the smaller doors to each room. The heavy hardware on the doors was made of plated silver. The mantels and hearths in all of the rooms were of finest Italian marble.

As neighbors gathered to watch the construction, wise ones must have wondered how the young couple could afford such elegance, even though Sarah Howard did bring a dowry of $30,000, as was rumored. Long before the mansion was completed, the public dubbed it "Matt's folly." In later years the Evans house came to be known as Sherwood Hall, in memory of its third owner, Sherwood C. Lindsay.

On May 8, 1835, before their house was ready for occupancy, a daughter was born to the Evanses whom they christened Augusta Jane, after her uncle Augustus Howard and her grandmother Jane (Vivian) Howard.[8] The birthplace of Augusta was Wildwood, probably a visitors' cottage near the great house. It is a shame that the circumstances of Augusta's birth could not accommodate an incorrect legend that she was born at the house which was later named St. Elmo, the home of her Aunt Mary Jones. This dignified old house, still one of Columbus' show places, would make a fitting background for the novelist's career, for Augusta's books contain many nostalgic descriptions of the gentle way of life in these spacious houses. At the time of her birth, however, her parents were visiting her Uncle John H. Howard, not her Aunt Mary.

While Matt and Sarah Evans were building Sherwood Hall, between 1834 and 1836, Columbus was at the height of its early boom. The high price of cotton (always an index to prosperity or depression in the South) and the profits of speculation in Indian lands over in Alabama had financed many civic improvements, as well as a score of costly mansion houses—those characteristic symbols of culture and affluence in the ante-bellum South, with their fluted columns, great verandas, formal gardens and evergreen trees. The children of the gentry were sent to one of the private academies. Drama came to Columbus about this time, when Sol Smith built a theatre in four days so that he could exhibit his itinerant stock company in *Pizarro,* the Indian roles to be taken by native Creeks from the reservations across the river. An historian records that at one performance the Indians drank too much whiskey and took charge of the show, inserting war-whoops and brandishing tomahawks; finally, the script was forgotten entirely when the Creeks fell into a noisy, droning war dance which lasted for hours.

Flush times brought the usual rowdy forms of amusement that accompanied a frontier settlement. Lamar's *Enquirer* reports many arrests for drunkenness and eye-gouging. The chief sport at the celebration of

Independence Day was the fighting of cocks, bouts beginning on July first, with finals on the evening of the fourth. One early historian remarks that in spite of the inspiration of the fine new Field School, the favorite sport of the boys was locking out the teacher, well knowing that if a holiday was gained without the teacher's dismissing the class himself, he would get his pay for the day—and perhaps punishments would be less severe.

In early childhood Augusta Evans saw the kind of life which a modern novelist would consider invaluable in the development of a future author. Long visits were made to the farmhouse in Alabama, where log rollings, corn huskings, house raisings, pig killings alternated with syllabub parties, barn dances, breakdowns by slaves, and concerts on the river steamers to supply amusement for the planter families of "the valley." In later years, if Augusta had chosen to be a realistic novelist instead of a domestic sentimentalist, she could have drawn upon incidents of which she and her relatives were eye-witnesses, in a period as exciting as our country has ever known. In addition to the wealth of materials from her childhood, she could have used more effectively the dramatic history which surrounded her adolescence and young womanhood — migration to Texas in a covered wagon, a ring-side seat during the war with Mexico, and personal services to the Confederacy. A portion of this fresh realism found its place in her Victorian novels, though lavendered with the peculiar dignity and moralizing of the times.

The first challenge to the security and prosperity

of Matt Evans and his fellow merchants in Columbus came with the depredations of the Creek and Cherokee Indians, who had resented their summary dismissal to reservations across the Chattahoochee.[9] Authorities in the new city allowed the red men to cross the river by daylight for trading purposes, but it was unlawful for an Indian to remain in Columbus after dark. Incidents were constantly occurring between the races; planters, traders, and itinerant preachers were attacked almost weekly. The whites, however, were not blameless. The lamentable plight of most Indians along the Chattahoochee between 1830 and 1836 rendered them easy victims to the frauds of unscrupulous land agents and impatient white planters who refused to await the successive dates appointed for the gradual evacuation of Indians westward. In addition, small-pox and cholera, poor crops, scarcity of game, and excessive drinking reduced hundreds of Creeks and Cherokees to begging on the streets of Columbus. Soon the Indians were attacking isolated settlements in large bands; numerous river steamers and stagecoaches were fired upon.

In February, 1836, panic seized the whites in the valley, and two thousand hysterical refugees crowded into Columbus. On the appeals of the Governors of Georgia and Alabama, President Jackson ordered General Winfield Scott (the handsome hero of our war with Mexico ten years later) and 1,200 militia to Columbus. Already mustered were the Columbus Guards (in which Matt Evans served as private), the Muscogee Blues, and three other local companies of guardsmen. Within two months the warlike Indians who refused to move westward were captured or driven away from the Chattahoochee. In 1837, a full year before the date agreed upon in earlier treaties, the troops completed the removal of the Indians to new lands beyond the Mississippi.

While the citizens and planters of the valley were bracing themselves for the showdown with the Indians, the remainder of the country was gripped by a severe economic depression. The prospect of opening new lands in the vacated reservations brought a fresh wave of speculation and inflation to Columbus, and the ravages of low prices and unemployment were postponed in this frontier town for several years. By the year 1838, the population within the city limits had increased to 4,121 (2,549 whites and 1,572 negroes). Colonel Seaborn Jones even solicited funds for a railroad into Columbus, at a time when most of the nation was suffering from serious panic. The great modern industries of Columbus, later operated by electric power generated on the river, had their modest beginning in John H. Howard's little Columbus Factory, the power for which was taken from the small dam that was supported by a tree cut down and thrown across a gorge.[10]

The early forties brought tragedy and business depression to Columbus. In March, 1841, the "Harrison freshet" (so named because it occurred at the time of William Henry Harrison's inauguration) washed away the great covered bridge over the river and destroyed buildings and crops throughout Muscogee and Russell counties. The scheme to connect Columbus with the

Western and Atlanta Railroad was abandoned during the year. In June, 1843, cotton was selling for two and one-half cents a pound, a price about one-half the cost of raising the staple.

Indicative of the unsettled times is Matt Evans's change of business: he became secretary (though he was not a director) of the Muscogee Insurance Company. The high cost of his house and lands was a contributing cause of his failure, but the bankruptcy of M. R. Evans & Company came soon after the purchase of $50,000 worth of dry goods, which had to be sold at far less than cost.[11]

Some idea of the affluence of the Evans family at this time can be gained from the items which are listed in the foreclosed mortgage on the estate, the document being originally executed on March 5, 1839: there were one hundred and forty-three acres of land at Sherwood Hall, and the family house, slave quarters, and barns; thirty-six slaves "together with the future increase of the same" were mortgaged along with a pleasure carriage, a pair of bay horses, three wagons, six mules, two farm horses, three cows, twenty-one large pieces of mahogany furniture, thirty-eight chairs, eight large carpets ("1 Welton, 3 Brussels, and 4 Scholcheds") and eight small rugs to match, one set of chinaware, and eighty-seven assorted pieces of silverware. All of these things, as well as the store, were lost in the bankruptcy. The mortgage was given to Matt's brother-in-law, Seaborn Jones, who had previously endorsed several notes of an earlier date.[12] It is likely that the worldly goods of Matt Evans were sold at public auction, since there is no evidence that any of his possessions remained in the Jones or Evans families. His house and lands in Georgia were acquired by General Armstrong Bailey. The impoverished Evans family was moved to a modest plantation house at Oswitchee in Russell County, Alabama.

The tensions of Augusta Jane Evans's childhood help to explain her preoccupation as a novelist with the theme of a strong-minded woman who is forced to combat the privations and slights which accompany poverty. As a precocious child of ten, she had experienced the confusion of unsettled social relationships in a pioneer town, the fears of Indian raids, and the embarrassment which attended her father's business failure and loss of their magnificent estate. Thirty years later, when the sale of her books brought her a fortune in excess of $100,000, she refused to invest her money in any firm which accepted mortgages on private dwellings. Still haunted by the fear of an empty purse in emergency, Mrs. Wilson always carried a hundred dollars on her person.

Augusta's childhood, however, was disciplined in various kinds of experience besides calamity. Her wise mother, though busy with the care of babies who arrived every two years, found time to instruct Augusta until she reached intellectual maturity. Poetry, history and geography were her favorite subjects, and the serious little scholar memorized her lessons without effort. In later years her thousands of readers marveled at the liberal use of obscure erudition and apt poetic quotations in her books, a practice which her critics and parodists often cited as her most annoying mannerism, but the author indignantly contradicted the charge that she kept an open encyclopedia beside her when she composed. The truth was that Augusta was gifted with that rare and dangerous asset, a photographic memory, which enabled her to retain verbatim the texts of many passages. Her early craving for books was fairly well satisfied while the family remained near Columbus, for the titles which were not available at home were usually to be found in one of the libraries of her wealthy relatives. Late in life, the novelist told a reporter that her mother was forced to follow Charles Lamb's advice: "The best way to educate a girl is to let her browse in a well selected library."[13] There were many forbidden books in the Howard, Evans and Jones libraries, undoubtedly, but the novelist once confessed that throughout her life she never opened a book which she thought her mother would disapprove. Mrs. Evans's educational standards were apparently very liberal, for Augusta read widely in modern science and in the philosophical works to which she often applied the term "scepticism." When she became a successful author, Augusta showered lavish gifts upon her mother and frequently repeated the words which she wrote to Mary Forrest in 1860: "She is in every sense my Alma Mater, the one to whom I owe everything, and whom I reverence more than all else on earth."[14]

Certainly there were more normal influences in her childhood than books and emotional tensions. She must have spent hours with her Howard cousins in games of housekeeping and Indian ball around the large verandas.

Since her family had a place in the society of "quality folks," Augusta probably enjoyed that form of pride, perhaps dearer to children than to adults who have matured, which accompanies belonging to the best society; as a mature woman, however, she had no patience with it.

One amusing incident of her early childhood was often related by the novelist. When she was about three years old, her mother took her shopping in Columbus, and on their return home Mrs. Evans discovered that Augusta had snitched a pair of red shoes and had hidden them under her cloak. Mrs. Evans's scolding was difficult for the child to understand, for Augusta insisted that the shoes were for her baby brother "Bud," and that it could not be called stealing since she took them out of love for "Bud." The part of the recollection which Mrs. Wilson enjoyed most was the merchant's hearty laugh when she was required to return the shoes and ask his pardon. Howard Evans, her beloved "Bud," remained one of her closest companions until his death in 1908.

If money was often scarce in the Evans household, there were other things to console the bright, serious girl—parental sympathy with her ambitions, four active brothers and sisters, splendid flower gardens, and an earnest desire to succeed as a teacher or writer. When international success came, she was not in the classroom, but the popularity of her books owes more to her teaching than to the excellencies of her style.

Matt and Sarah Evans struggled against adverse conditions in Columbus until early in 1845, when they made a characteristic American decision: they would escape from their troubles at home by migrating westward. Ever since Lamar and Fannin had led scores of fellow Georgians to the battlefields of Texas, where each leader became a hero, the young men of Columbus had been urged to follow, and many did. During the spring of 1845 preparations were made to move the large Evans family and their modest household goods over the rough roads of the Gulf states to the Texas sheeplands. This decision is difficult to understand, since the area of Texas to which they were migrating was not only a center of operations for the war with Mexico, but was inhabited by hostile Mexicans and sullen Comanches, who had been linked with a succession of depredations upon settlers from the States.

CHAPTER III

San Antonio

1845-1849

"GONE TO TEXAS" became a stock answer to inquiries about transient Southerners in the thirties and forties. Economic insecurity, as in the case of Matt Evans, was the chief reason for migrating to an area so fraught with uncertainties, but the clamor of Southern leaders and newspapers to avenge Mexican insults to *our* honor attracted many adventurous men. These appeals stressed the importance of Americanizing the southern portion of Texas by permanent settlement, but the persuasive elements in the propaganda were the promises of wealth, glory and much animal fun to be had by all.

Matt Evans was known among his cronies as a light-hearted, songful goodfellow, whose youthful spirit would probably have succumbed to the "Texas fever" even if his business and possessions had not been lost in the downward swirl of depression. It was probably in the early summer of 1845 that his covered wagons set out on the long journey.[15] A yankee traveler, Frederick Olmsted, who passed over the same route nine years later, describes a typical party of Southern emigrants:

Several families were frequently moving together, coming from the

> same district, or chance met and joined for company on the long road from Alabama, Georgia, or the Carolinas. Before you come upon them you hear, ringing through the woods, the fierce cries and blows which they urge on their jaded cattle. . . One of these trains was made up of three large wagons, and a gang of twenty able field hands. They travel ten or fifteen miles a day, stopping wherever night overtakes them. The masters are plainly dressed, often in home-spun, keeping their eyes about them, noticing the soil, sometimes making a remark on the crops by the roadside; but, generally, dogged, surly, and silent. The women are silent, too, frequently walking to relieve the teams, and weary, haggard, mud be-draggled, forlorn, and disconsolate, yet hopeful and careful. The negroes, mud-incrusted, wrapped in old blankets or gunny-bags, suffering from cold, plod on, aimless, hopeless, thoughtless, more indifferent than the oxen to all about them.[16]

The most vivid recollection which Augusta retained of the journey to Texas was her mother's brightening the long hours with stories about great writers. She remembered particularly Mrs. Evans's enthusiastic recitations of the poetry of Cowper, whose sombre meditations upon religion, nature and humanity were a solace to the little band:

> God made the country, and man made the town.
> What wonder then that health and virtue, gifts
> That can alone make sweet the bitter draught
> That Life holds out to all, should most abound
> And least be threatened in the fields and groves?

This record of the untiring mother, who cared for five small children during an uncomfortable journey through an Indian-infested wilderness and yet found time to hear her eldest daughter's lessons and to instruct her in poetry, was one which Augusta Evans took pride in retelling throughout her life.

The Evans party arrived in Texas about the time that Americans everywhere were debating the wisdom of General Zackary Taylor's occupation of Corpus Christi, in the late summer of 1845. They remained in Houston several weeks until a sixth child was born, Mary Elizabeth, and then moved on to Galveston, where Matt left his family while he went farther south to investigate the rumor of free lands on the plains near San Antonio. The old Spanish town, long the junction of several thriving trade routes from Mexico to the Texas interior and to Gulf ports, was booming from a lively trade in materials of war.

It was probably January, 1846, when Matt Evans led his family southward to their new home. As the wagon train approached the northeastern outskirts of San Antonio, the first view which Augusta had of the town could hardly have conformed with the bookish ten-year-old's image of a pioneer Spanish settlement. She saw two rows of neatly constructed log-houses, the occupants of which were neither Spaniards, Mexicans, native Texans, nor Indians, but a group of German immigrants who had arrived within the last eighteen months.[17] While the Evans family resided in San Antonio, these Germans built prim little houses of creamy-white limestone, decorated with small bow windows and balconies, framed by pink window blinds.

The business district of San Antonio, already dominated by American merchants, lay within a bend of the San Antonio river, a stream praised by Augusta Evans and Olmsted for its clear blue water flowing rapidly over pebbles between reedy banks. Within easy walking distance of their commercial establishments, the aggressive Americans built simple frame houses, easily identified by their jalousies and white picket fences. At that time, the square of Alamo was predominantly Mexican, with several hundred windowless cabins nearby, all built of adobe blocks and roofed with river grass which the Mexicans called *tula*. Many of these flat dwellings were washed in blue or yellow. The business houses near the plaza revealed San Antonio's recent Americanization. Cheap frame structures, housing American hotels, stood adjacent to old stone buildings of Spanish architecture, now converted by gaudy carpentry into saloons, called *exchanges*. The grim, ancient stuccoed cathedral, suggesting the city's European heritage, stood in contrast to the glass-fronted stores, often cut out of old Spanish walls.

Five years later Augusta attempted to describe the streets of San Antonio in her first novel, *Inez*, which she undertook at the age of fifteen. The reader is impressed with the impulsive girl's enthusiasm for the colorful city, but her stilted allusions and excited Byronic generalities tell us little about the place:

> Although a strict analysis might prove detrimental, I assure you the *tout ensemble* was picturesque indeed.
>
> "Italia! oh Italia! thou hast
> The fatal gift of beauty."
>
> art rivaled here! Thy gorgeous skies have floated hither, and hover like a halo round the town.[18]

A far more satisfactory account of San Antonio, written about five years after Augusta lived there, is found in Olmsted's homely details. The yankee tourist describes the sauntering or idle Mexican males and their animated olive-skinned women, whose "dresses seemed lazily reluctant to cover their plump persons, and their attitudes were always expressive of the influence of a Southern sun upon national manners." Efficent bearded German merchants and ranchmen mingled with stalking silent Comanche Indians and bustling yankees—a conglomeration of nationalities and races, all doing business together, though suspiciously, under the blazing Texas sun. Olmsted says of San Antonio of 1854:

> We [in the United States] have no city, except perhaps New Orleans, that can vie in point of picturesque interest that attaches to odd and antiquated foreignness, with San Antonio. Its jumble of races, costumes, languages and buildings; its religious ruins . . . its remote, isolated, outposted situation, and the vague conviction that it is the first of a new class of conquered cities into whose decaying streets our rattling life is to be infused, combine with the heroic touches in its history to enliven and satisfy your traveler's curiosity.[19]

The fame of San Antonio had become international since the tragic martyrdom of its patriots at the Alamo. With the declaration of war against Mexico on May 13, 1846, the city became one of the most important depots for military supplies in all Texas, although it had long been a thriving trading center. Shortly after the Evans family arrived, the city's small population of about 2,500 was taxed to accommodate the hundreds of troops who were assembling there. The Tennessee and Kentucky cavalries, ordered to reinforce General Zackary Taylor after the victory at Monterey, were delayed in San Antonio longer than was expected.

The presence of the troops, with their reassuring stacks of ammunition and supplies, naturally gave the San Antonians a feeling of security, even though the town was more vulnerable to attack and occupation than any other large settlement north of the Neuces River. Not even the imprudent march of Brevet Colonel Harney out from San Antonio and across the Rio Grande in September, 1846, and his subsequent retreat from Mexico with embarrassing losses of men, supplies and prestige, impressed the Texans with the possibility of a Mexican victory. But south of the Rio Grande there was far less fear of American armies than Texans assumed at the time. The American standing army was held in contempt by Mexican officers, and our vacillating foreign policies and continuous internal dissensions convinced Mexican politicians that we could never unite against them. One intelligent Mexican journal, *Il Siglo,* expressed the anti-American sentiment in these words: "[An American is] a being detestable to the nation on account of the little accord between [him and] the religion, the language, and the gentle, affable, frank and generous character of the Mexican."[20]

Many recent arrivals in San Antonio had come from communities which were unacquainted with the Catholic clergy. They openly accused the Roman Church of supporting the cause of Catholic Mexico in 1845, as other Protestants had suspected in the battles of 1836. Since local Mexicans and Indians had old grievances against Protestant Americans who had coveted the rich plains of southern Texas, and since the Jesuit Fathers had great influence among the Latins and redmen, it was natural to suspect that this influence supplied the link between the original inhabitants of San Antonio and the Mexican authorities.

In her *Inez, a Tale of the Alamo,* Augusta develops melodramatically the theme of Jesuit assistance to Mexico in the Texas War of Independence. She creates in Mazzolin a villainous Jesuit who serves as Santa Anna's spy before the fall of the Alamo, and who is allowed to say that he hopes to see "hundreds of these cursed [Texan] heretics" slain by the invading Mexican armies. The youthful authoress did not make use of similar tensions and suspicions of the year 1846, but she did attack the work of the Catholic clergy in the earlier war with such vigor and earnestness that one wonders if she is not revealing the fears and excitement of the later conflict which she knew intimately.

Though war had brought many varieties of uncertainty to San Antonio since the arrival of the Evans family, the town continued to enjoy good trade. Sometime in 1846 Mr. Evans made a connection with a mercantile firm within the city and acquired an interest in a sheep ranch.[21] There is no record that his firm was among the lucky contractors and merchants who prospered by supplying the army of General Taylor (several agents established comfortable permanent fortunes), but business in his small store was good enough to keep him in San Antonio during three years of insecurity and bloodshed.

In a letter to Mary Forrest, written about 1858, Augusta Evans recalled her adolescent impressions of the old city:

I remember rambling about the crumbling walls of the Alamo, recalling all its bloody horrors; and as I climbed the moldering, melancholy pile, to watch the last rays of the setting sun gild the hill-tops, creep down the sides, and slowly sink into the blue waves of the San Antonio River: as I looked over the quietly beautiful valley, with its once noble Alameda of stately cottonwoods, my heart throbbed, and I wondered if I should be able some day to write about it for those who had never looked upon a scene so fair. I seem even now to be winding once more through that lovely valley, holding my mother's hand tightly, as she repeated beautiful descriptions from Thomson's *Seasons* and Cowper's *Task;* again I see the white flock slowly descending the hills, and bleating as they wound home to my father's fold.[22]

In the exciting year 1849, when thousands of Americans were rushing westward across the plains and Rockies to seek gold in California, Matt Evans made the kind of decision which our historians often neglect to record: he rejected the promise of western pioneering and prepared to return eastward, to renew a life which he understood, among people who knew him. His descendants say that the discomforts of frontier life and the numerous instances of violence near San Antonio, more than commercial failure, drove him to this decision. Contemporary records of San Antonio and southeastern Texas give us ample evidence of the reasons which prompted him to remove his wife and six small children from the troubled area.

The hard-drinking Mexicans of San Antonio habitually galloped their horses through the streets, reckless of pedestrians. Almost weekly, the stage drivers and traders reported attacks upon white Texans by Indians or Mexicans. Quarrels occurred continually over runaway slaves, who were protected or captured and resold by scheming redmen and their confederates south of the border. Rumors were often heard in San Antonio of Indians being incited by Mexicans to settle old scores with the conquering white men. Massacres and depredations were not new to the Evanses, but it was one thing to experience them while living among dozens of relatives and within call of a well trained militia, and quite another to live among hostile Indians and Mexicans, far from relatives and without adequate means of defense.

If Mrs. Evans and Augusta pleaded with Matt Evans to take the family back to Alabama, the Comanches furnished them with a most convincing argument in their brutal practice of holding captives, particularly women and children, for ransom. During the late forties, agents and travelers in Indian territory reported that some tribes held as many as five hundred whites in a state of slavery. Tragic accounts were brought to San Antonio of the tortures inflicted upon Mrs. Horn, Cynthia Ann Parker, Mrs. Plummer, Matilda Lockhard, and scores of other white women and children, some of whom were raped by the savage warriors; others were pinched, beaten and forced to perform hard labors. Several mothers saw their infants thrown into the air and crushed to death as they fell. One woman reported that she was strapped to a half-wild horse and carried on a long journey.

The dangers and privations of frontier life were disturbing enough, but other traits of San Antonio's colorful life were especially shocking to the devout and conventional Sarah Evans and her precocious elder daughter. Olmsted observed that American Protestants in the town had become indifferent to their church obligations. Also, the Southern ladies could not be expected to view the evidence of moral laxity among the Mexican women with the same amusement as did the robust yankee traveler, who remarked that the senoritas were very gay and wore their chemises "as low as possible in the neck, sometimes even lower." Unashamed consorting of Mexicans and Negroes offended Southern slaveholders. The presence of a very active Catholic clergy, whose tenets and influence had long aroused suspicions among prevailingly Protestant landowners in the South, disturbed Augusta so deeply that she attacked them vigorously in her first novel, an act which she regreted later when a friendship with a scholarly nun, Sister Mary Stanislaus, modified this prejudice.

The solution of the Indian question back in Georgia and Alabama, in which Matt Evans had taken an active part, was quite simple: the Cherokees, Choctaws and Creeks were requested to move west of the Mississippi, and those who failed to obey were escorted to their new home by the militia, abetted by the U.S. Army. Texans were late in applying such simple tactics. In the forties there was plenty of land in Texas for both races, provided they did not violate each other's customs. Using his rifle as his best argument, the white Texan kept the Indian at bay — most of the time. However, the nomadic Comanches and Kiowas were slow to accept the white man's views on land ownership. For centuries these wandering tribes had ranged hundreds of miles beyond the borders of Texas and returned to the South at will, as the various seasons offered supplies of game. The white man's habit of fencing in his land, or declaring his ownership of vast expanses of open pasture by posting it against trespassers, was puzzling to the Indians. Unfortunately for the whites who lived in such exposed localities as San Antonio, the Indians' economic philosophy was bolstered by effective propaganda from Mexican officials and spies.

The recollection of their short-lived prosperity in Columbus, as well as the violence of the West, prompted the Evanses to load their covered wagons again and get off letters to friends in Alabama. In her early novels Augusta Evans often created the kind of "good life" which her father had dreamed of, and the young woman's views probably reflect the prejudices of her parents, particularly those of Mrs. Evans, her tutor and confidante. If so, they hoped to acquire again such elements in the Southern way of life as the willing surrender of household chores to slaves, a faith in continued economic and personal security, respect for family ties and family influence, reverence for long established codes of conduct, and unquestioned acceptance of class and racial distinctions. Such undebatable assurances—at least in the mind of a Southern matron—met harsh and stubborn resistance in San Antonio. The successful Western pioneer was no less chivalrous than the Southern Bourbon, but the views and objects of their reverence were often far apart. Like so many Southerners since their time, the Evanses felt that a life amid people whose familiar responses could be counted upon, a life dependent upon long accepted and neatly simplified economic patterns, was preferable even in genteel poverty to the insecure democratic gusto of Western empire-building.

In the early summer of 1849 Matt Evans turned his horses homeward and tramped through the wet marshes and lush forest toward Mobile.

CHAPTER IV

Mobile and Inez

1849-1855

IN THE SUMMER of 1849 Mobile offered many things to homesick Southerners like the Evanses. The small Gulf port had grown and prospered steadily in spite of panics in the thirties and forties. Its wharves now received annually several hundred thousand bales of river-borne "white gold" from Alabama's Black Belt. The most ambitious commercial development of its history was about to be realized: the construction of a railroad five hundred miles long, which would open the back country of Alabama, Mississippi, Tennessee, Arkansas and Kentucky, and start the flow of goods and wealth from the Ohio River to the Gulf. A stupendous undertaking for a little city of about 20,000, one-third of whom were negro slaves.[23]

This great venture had been nourished by the fanatical interest of a single man, Marshall J. D. Baldwyn, who in spite of ridicule had argued that the city was destined to handle a million bales of cotton annually, if the merchants would only back his scheme. Early in '49 Southern capitalists finally accepted "Baldwyn's folly" as a rich possibility, and their plans were broadcast in newspapers over the entire nation. Stocks and bonds of the "M. & O." were placed on sale.

Out in San Antonio, Matt Evans heard reports of the great boom that would accompany the building of the Mobile and Ohio Railroad. He seized this chance to return homeward and to seek again the peace of mind and economic security which Texas had failed to give his family. Augusta's literary ambitions would find a more fertile soil in the old colonial city. Her mother's tutoring had developed a deep love of books and an insatiable curiosity, but now she was ready to discuss the forms of literature which her mother was unprepared to analyze—critical articles in the latest English quarterlies and treatises on esthetics and metaphysics. Mrs. Evans even dreamed of placing Augusta in one of the academies for young ladies, if Mr. Evans found remunerative employment. Also, there would be zealous Methodists in Mobile, and fewer street brawls, and no savage Comanches. Most consoling of all, the Evanses would be eight hundred miles nearer the hospitable mansions of relatives and friends in Columbus.

On their arrival in Mobile Matt Evans rented a modest cottage in the piney woods a little distance from the city and found employment as a factor with a cotton merchant. Apparently he had moderate success for a time, for Augusta was sent to a private school until she was forced to withdraw because of poor health; again Mrs. Evans became her tutor. Matt Evans had sufficient means to become a member of Mobile's most convivial club, the Cowbellion de Rakin Society, a group of men who dedicated themselves to the proper celebration of New Year's Day. The Cowbellions were organized spontaneously on January 1, 1831, when a tipsy crowd of celebrants, led by Michael Krafft, raided a hardware store and appropriated enough garden rakes and cow-bells to make their enthusiasm heard throughout the town. Their name and coat-of-arms were taken from the implements which they removed from the Barney-Cavanagh Company.[24]

Misfortunes and increased responsibilities soon caught up with Matt Evans. Late in 1849 a fire destroyed the house he rented and much personal property was lost. In the early fifties his health began to fail, and his family suffered once more from frequent losses in salary. These burdens were made doubly severe by the high cost of living in the boom town. In the fall of 1850 there were eight children in the Evans household: Augusta aged fifteen, Howard thirteen, Vivian ten, Caroline eight, Sarah six, Mary Elizabeth five, Randolph two, and Virginia an infant born on August sixth.

The humiliations of poverty which had plagued the family for ten years made a lasting impression upon Augusta. Within twenty-five years she was to become one of the wealthiest women in Alabama, but in book after book she continued to depict the kinds of hardships which she had known so intimately. Apparently the American public did not tire of the story of a precocious girl of fragile health who is forced to sacrifice valuable time from her writing (or music or painting) in order to support herself and her relatives. As was true also with Augusta, the heroines of her novels were usually burdened with an additional obligation, accepted willingly and cheerfully, of nursing the sick.

When successive epidemics of yellow fever ravaged the low-lying residential areas of Mobile in the early fifties, the only trained nurses available to assist the doctors were a few Catholic nuns. Augusta's steely will, her energy and native competence were discovered by herself at this time, and she set about the task of making herself indispensable beside many a sickbed. Vivid descriptions of the pestilence and of the work of volunteer nurses—among the most realistic passages she ever wrote—were later incorporated into chapters seventeen and eighteen of *Beulah.*

Augusta would have considered a fee for her services as an affront. Several years later, her proficiency and fame as a volunteer nurse brought about two of the most cherished events of her life. First, in recognition of her services as a Confederate nurse, she received an elegantly written commendation and a diamond-studded pen from the great strategist, General P. G. T. Beauregard. Later, through her kindly assistance at the bedside of a relative, she developed a friendship with her wealthy neighbor, Colonel Lorenzo Madison Wilson, who became her husband.

Domestic problems and a fervent interest in the troubles of humanity hampered Augusta's preparation for authorship, but she accepted them without complaint or apology. Because of the frequent illness of her father, she probably would have welcomed some kind of commercial employment for herself, but Southern traditions placed a strict limitation upon the kinds of work which a daughter of "quality folks" could accept. She nourished a secret hope that her parents' respect for literature would overcome any opposition they might have to her accepting money for writing. School teaching was considered, but she had no diploma from a respectable school as proof of her ability.

Augusta worked out her problem alone. She was well aware of the moral stigma often attached to *novels* in that day, but she planned to give her own composition such religious fervor that any opposition to the form would quickly disappear among her readers. Since she was not sure of the opinions of her parents, she took only one person into her confidence, an old colored slave named Minervy. Each night the old Negro found enough oil to light Augusta's lamp until the early hours; each morning she helped destroy evidences of the night's labors and found a safe hiding place for the manuscript.

Years later Mrs. Wilson often told her friends about the exposure of this conspiracy with Minervy. The faithful servant began to worry about Augusta's health, for when Minervy arrived before daylight to prepare the bread for breakfast, she heard Augusta stirring in the room above. Intent upon not betraying the young lady directly, Minervy went to Mrs. Evans with this story, according to a letter by Augusta's best friend, Mrs. Rachel Lyons Heustis:

> "Miss, you's always worrying about that Augusta Jane, and a-complaining she's so weakly, and don't eat nothing, and nothing I cooks don't suit her, and there ain't no reason on this yearth for it, but because she is too *perlitical*!"

"Too perlitical! Why, what do you mean?"

"Well, ma'am, it is just that she is too perlitical. I sees her light a-burning every morning of the world 'fore day, when I is making out my rolls, and Sylvy say her lamp done burn clean empty every day; and I tells you she is 'tirely too perlitical!"[26]

During an interview with Augusta, accompanied with much squirming and many endeavors to avoid confession, Mrs. Evans heard about the book she was writing. It was agreed between them that Mr. Evans should not hear about *Inez, A Tale of the Alamo* until the ambitious project was completed. Finally, on Christmas morning of 1854, Augusta presented the neatly copied manuscript to her father as a gift. It would have been difficult for such a convivial spirit as Matt Evans to oppose his teen-age daughter's subtle strategy.

Augusta chose to unify her historical materials by depicting the adventures of a group of emigrants to Texas who were destined to play heroic parts in several battles of the Texas War of Independence. As a child she had often heard the exciting stories which the people of Columbus told about Lamar, Fannin and their followers. These adventures make the climax of *Inez*, but there are also lovers in the story, and a number of other quaint things. The sheltered Puritan authoress was incapable of responding to the demands of her story, particularly the love theme. Likewise, the violence and treachery associated with Goliad and the Alamo could be revealed only in such stilted, self-conscious language as,

One hundred and fifty brave hearts poured out their life-blood by [Travis's] motionless form, struck down like sheep in the slaughter-pen. But seven remained; in despair they gazed on the ruin around, reeling from exhaustion and slipping in gore. There was borne on the midnight air a faint, feeble cry: "Quarter! quarter!" Alas! brave hearts, the appeal was lost, for an incarnate demon led the thirsty band. With a fiendish yell it was answered back, "No quarter!" and ye seven were stretched beside yon fearless, noble Travis![27]

One portion of the struggle for Texas independence was of particular interest to Augusta at this time, and she considered herself especially qualified to analyze it: the dangers of Catholicism in that old Mexican province and the contrasting virtues of Protestantism, as she had been taught to see them. A large portion of the Americans who had migrated to Texas were from areas of the South where Catholicism was not well established. This was especially true of the Evans family. Within a few years Augusta experienced an ordeal of doubt and confusion in her religious beliefs, from which she emerged with a greater tolerance for the creeds of all denominations.

The religious propaganda of this juvenile novel is developed in the efforts of two noble women to thwart the schemes of a villainous Jesuit, whose support of Mexico during the war and whose zeal in behalf of his church are attacked as evils of equal stature. The author strives to enlist the reader's sympathy for the Texans through Inez's adventurous exploits in thwarting Mazzolin's political wickedness. The campaign against the errors in Catholic doctrine is conducted mainly through long harangues by the gentle Mary, who seeks to avert the conversion of a childhood friend to Roman faith.

Miss Evans's inventory of Catholic errors includes most of the timeworn charges. Priests are mercenary and often commit physical cruelties when opposed. Many of the non-Protestant doctrines of Catholicism are akin to superstition, and since Catholics are denied the right to analyze their beliefs, they commit their consciences "to the care of the priest." The Catholic Church, the heroine argues, keeps its strong hold upon ignorant minds by fostering a belief in the latter-day miracles of its priests, saints and relics. And finally, we are told that priests use "unknown tongues" and a kind of hypnotism to bring about their mesmeric control over their flocks, a charge which was frequently heard at that time.

The zealous teen-age authoress did not confine herself to these non-rational charges, some as weird as an old wives' tale. She believed that the foundations of Catholicism must be examined, and like a modern Red Cross Knight armed with reason, she permits the heroine to tackle some of the most abstruse problems of theology, citing book and passage in her refutations. The form of the confession is analyzed and condemned. Catholic reverence for their saints, particularly the belief that the saints can intercede for the sinner and aid in the absolution of sins, is exposed as an injury to the mediative position of Christ. A religious conflict of more recent date is brought into the argument when the author suggests that the evil influences of "Puseyism" and "Latitudinarianism" among Protestants is attributable to Catholic propaganda.

It is easy to visualize the young scholar's search for arguments in this great conflict, as she conceived it to be. Very likely her Methodist minister helped to find the sources for her and then criticized the results. But more important than an identification of her guides or an exposure of the weaknesses in her argument, is an understanding of the patterns of thought which prompted her to interlard an historical novel with a savage attack upon an influential institution. Every grave and earnest Victorian who followed her examination of the issue was in sympathy with her determination to take an unequivocal stand upon a vital question, though many must have questioned her logic. The study of history was among the most serious intellectual pursuits of the nineteenth century, but the necessity for taking a firm position on moral or ethical questions was regarded even more highly.

Most critics have agreed with a contemporary's estimate of *Inez* as a work of art: "There is not a natural character and scarcely a natural phrase in the whole volume."[28] A multitude of readers have been attracted to this "Tale of the Alamo" by its appealing title and by the reputation of later novels, particularly *Beulah* and *St. Elmo*. Writing of the appearance of *Inez* "in a handsome duodecimo volume" in 1867, Davidson states that the novel "impresses one just as *The Professor*—[Charlotte Bronte's] first dreadful failure—when republished upon the strength of the author's reputation, won by other, later, and better works."[29]

Harper accepted *Inez,* in spite of its weaknesses, though this established firm probably received a subsidy large enough to cover the costs of one edition. Several prominent Mobilians have been mentioned as the "angel" of *Inez,* but the donor was probably Augustus Howard, the novelist's uncle and namesake. The frail little novel appeared anonymously in 1855, when Augusta was in her twentieth year. A surprising number of editions of *Inez* have been published in the last ninety-five years. Eight publishers were offering a total of fourteen issues of it in 1912, fifty-seven years after its appearance, and four houses listed six issues in the year 1928. It is still in print.

The next ten years, 1856-1866, so fertile intellectually throughout the Western world, brought many challenges to Augusta. She matched her Methodist Fundamentalism against "Speculation," and the victory which she won, as outlined in *Beulah,* was accepted by herself and her ardent readers as a mighty blow for righteousness. She fell in love with a man whose temperament was much like her own, but their intense loyalties to diverse political factions soon parted them, he to defend Lincoln with stirring editorials in the New York *Times,* she to become a very effective propagandist, as well as war nurse, for the South. Augusta marched in the ranks of the Confederacy as militantly as propriety would allow a lady to do in those times, but just two years after the defeat of the beloved cause, her spirit was still strong enough to achieve national acclaim with *St. Elmo.*

Good mentors prepared her for these stirring events: adversity, wide reading, common sense, recognition of her own limitations, and especially a thoughtful young preacher who shaped her thinking. It is doubtful that her circle of friends was very large before 1859. She would undoubtedly have enjoyed the spirited conversation at the salon of a famous Mobile authoress and world traveler, Madame Octavia Walton Le Vert, but there is no evidence that she was ever invited. The glamorous Octavia had inspired Washington Irving to say, "Such a woman occurs but once in the course of an Empire." Her popular *Souvenirs of Travel* (1859) was suggested by the great Frenchman, Lamartine, who described her as a "natural *improvisatrice*." Madame Le Vert must have been a remarkable raconteur, but her advantages were prodigious compared to the background of Augusta Evans: Octavia's grandfather, George Walton, signed the Declaration of Independence; her father, the Governor of the Territory of Florida, permitted her to select the name for the capital, Tallahassee, meaning "beautiful land"; besides Irving, her close friends in New York and Washington were such people as Calhoun, Clay, Webster and Nathaniel P. Willis; and she was once lavishly entertained by the Duke of Rutland. Perhaps Augusta's inability to move in such fashionable and brilliant circles during her formative years had something to do with her bitter attacks upon the *beau monde* in most of her books, but there is no evidence that the activities of Madame Le Vert were resented by Augusta—except the invitations extended by the Le Verts to yankee officers after the fall of Mobile.[30]

CHAPTER V

Speculation versus Fundamentalism

1855-1859

"Verily, I am a mystery unto myself"

Ours is "the Reflective or Philosophical age," boasted Emerson, but intellectuals of later generations have sometimes rewarded these confident words with a smile. In those years of turbulent idealism, there were scores of contemporaries of the great sage of Concord, some honored and others merely ambitious, who caught the oracular message and believed it. Bravely, earnestly they sought to prove that it was fashionable to think. Were not the masters of the age publicizing their spiritual ordeals and their reactions to science in dramatic rhetoric — Goethe, Coleridge, Wordsworth, Carlyle, Tennyson, Cardinal Newman, Arnold, Emerson, Thoreau, Melville, Whitman, Lanier and others? Even Lord Byron had posed as a philosopher as he "bore the pageant of his bleeding heart through Europe."

Augusta Jane Evans was steeped in the works of these great men, and like some of them she believed that she had a mission in life. If her art was inferior to theirs, her zeal for the right prompted her to insert messages in her novels which would be ample apology for her art. The erudition in her writing indicates that she hoped to attract intellectual readers, but when it became evident that the masses and not the intelligentsia were her constituents, she professed to be pleased that her audience was composed of unsophisticated commoners who follow the dictates of their heart and conscience, even in matters of art.

Her adolescent tilt with Catholicism led Augusta into a frenzied and honest examination of her own beliefs, most of which were the foundations of the evangelical Protestantism which her devout mother had taught her to revere. This ordeal of scepticism was an unnerving experience to the sober young scholar, but she met it with the same bravery and frankness which characterized her literary idols. In reading her letters of the period, and particularly her fictional confession in *Beulah,* modern readers may feel embarrassment before the self consciousness and rhapsody of her prose, but to accept these materials as Miss Evans's generation understood them, we must overcome the time lag and restore the fervor and sincerity with which our ancestors faced the drama of faith and doubt. Those willing to bring such "poetic faith" to *Beulah* or *St. Elmo* may even find grounds for pardoning the extravagant sentimentalism in the language of these best sellers.

In her search for refutations of Catholic doctrines Augusta met a scholarly young Methodist preacher, the Reverend Walter Harriss, who directed her theological studies in preparation for *Inez* and rendered calm assistance in her quest for a satisfactory Christian faith. Many impulsive letters, confessions of doubt concerning the very foundations of Christianity, were directed to this "dear friend and brother."[31]

Apparently Augusta's mother listened with confident detachment to any troubled doubts which the young woman was willing to confide in her. We learn from Augusta's letters that she read aloud for hours to Mrs. Evans, with interpolated comments, from the books which multiplied her original doubts—such works as *Hours with the Mystics,* the *Theologia Germanica,* Mills' *Logic,* and Hoty's translation of Gobineau's *Moral and Intellectual Diversities of the Races* [*Essai sur L'inégalité des Races Humaines*]. No mention is made in these letters of her mother's alarm over her speculations.

The youthful sceptic's correspondence suggests that her problem was perhaps more emotional than ecclesiastical, that her doubt created a nervous unrest which intensified her intellectual uncertainty. She writes about "the inscrutable mystery" of her soul's relation to God on the one hand and to the earth on the other. "Why are these things?" she pleads. "A mocking echo that fell back with a dead crushing weight upon my sickened heart" was the only answer she found to her questionings. She tells her friend that she "resolved to come to some definite conclusion" because she could not remain "at that grim goal of speculation where I believed nothing! And only those whose souls have been thus wrung, and tortured, and well nigh deadened can fully appreciate the intensity of my mental struggles." For a time she found release in nature. "I laid my weary aching head, yearningly, upon the great throbbing heart of Mother Nature! I went out of myself! Out! Out among God's witnesses and listened to their undertones." They told her that earthly experiences are inexact, that she could never know the final answers in this world. They counseled her to "have done with taunting sophisms, and golden tissued-webs of philosophy. And high soaring peculations, that but build you Godless altars heaven-high, and then dash you back to grovel in deeper night. Trust God! and be at peace."

When she thought that she was near the end of her struggle and believed that she would rest securely on "the rock of Ages," Augusta was able to view her mighty battle with calm detachment. Her soul, she confesses to Mr. Harriss, had gone "clean through that slough of mis-called philosophy" and had come out on the other side. She was now ready to reject the atheistic metaphysicians who wrangle on concerning the question of proof in religion. She can now agree with Carlyle that the "black smoke as of Tophet" which represents our doubt of God's favor, may through our "heart energy" become a flame of Heaven. She cries out to her confessor:

> Courage! But there is only one well of heart-energy, and the windlass is in God's hand! We cannot draw at all times. No! No! Some thirsty spirits have to wait long. And then the longed-for draught seems all the sweeter. I have been sorely tried on many points. I do not pretend to be satisfied! I never expect to be in this world. But I am sick to death of the struggle. And impotent

to help myself, I give it over and admit that I do not and cannot know anything, save as God wills I should. Like a caged bird, I have quit fluttering madly against the bars, and am waiting for the appointed hours, when food is to be given my soul. Where is the sense of beating yourself to death, unavailingly. You can't help yourself and you will eventually have to do as I have done. My proud nature you know . . . and imagine what a fierce bitter conflict it cost me ere I could bring my spirit to rest on the Ararat of dependence of "blind faith." Whether I shall stay there is now the question. I seem to hear afar-off, the roar and mutter of those maddened waves that lashed me well-nigh to desperation. And I am afraid to creep down to the base of my resting place, lest they surge over me again. Like a sick child after a violent spasm, I am willing to be quiet, almost anywhere.

Since peace of mind accompanied her acceptance of "blind faith," she felt that the German Transcendentalists should be forgotten. "I rather think I shall let Fichte alone. What say you, my Brother? Shall I go down again to the brink and challenge a second storm?" And yet she wondered if her newly found peace was entirely adequate for her earthly needs: "There is a hope in God, you know, that is despair of life. And oh! I trust him."

Later, after she resolved to re-accept the creed of Methodism and hand in her letter to the church near her home in Summerville, she was able to write her friend:

My Brother, I am happy now! O so happy! I lift up my arms yearningly toward the clear loving sky that bends over me and feel that my heart cannot hold its deep joy! Sometimes, the very intensity and exquisiteness of feeling is painful. . . . My friend, do not set me down as a silly rhapsodist! I am in earnest! And only wish you could enjoy this spring-time of my soul with me. "What is the nature of this feeling?" I hear you ask. Why it is as if my God, my great all-Father, were speaking to me from every flower and tree, every cloudlet that flecks the sky, every wandering breath of air that fans my brow. O! all Nature is a grand musical instrument, whose key-notes are "God" and "Labor." And in humble gratitude I say, my own organ of heart-strings makes no discord in the universal harmony. It is as though a great well-spring of strength "bubbled at my feet, and I had drank, and drank, and thirsted no more."

In spite of a victory as joyous as Herr Teufelsdroech's in *Sartor Resartus,* the "ecstasy" of which she had written so confidently in the spring was challenged again in October. She thanked Mr. Harriss for his "counsel regarding church matters" (he had apparently insisted that she rejoin the church), but she hesitated still because she was uncertain of her faith.

There are seasons when my soul plumes itself for the lofty regions of speculation, and for a time I flutter among the bald cliffs and crags of a so-called "philosophic spiritualism" of intuitionalism, but I seem to freeze in those Artic heights, and my numb soul gladly warms itself in the sunny realms of God's holy revelation. Verily I am a mystery unto myself. Like a dazzled moth I hover round and round a brilliant spark that may one day consume me. I have not struggled through the morasses of skepticism without inhaling some of its deadly vapors. I mean that when my soul is serenely, happily basking in the light of an eternal God and his equally eternal word, a grim gaunt spectre stands by me as my shadow and makes me doubt the reasonable certainty and absolute proof of the faith that consoles me, and herein lies the curse of skepticism—that its ghostly battles have to be continually fought over and over. Blessed the soul that never began to question and debate regarding its arcana.

Augusta explained to her "Mentor" that she would never desert her faith again, but she could not help bemoaning "the constant desire to ask and be answered on theologic points," the restless longing for "logical certainty." Like the great Victorian poet, she believed that her "honest doubt" contained a validity as pious as "the dim verdicts that trembling faith utters."

Among the problems which troubled her (and many another hesitant agnostic of her time) were the articles of various denominations which contain contradictory elements—"so much that is distorted and sectariarially twisted," as she put it.

> But the question very naturally presents itself: "Who is in the right? There are direct antagonisms all drawn from the identical volume." Unitarians and Trinitarians have as yet only begun the discussion of that important point, and from all I can see of the subject it seems pretty well balanced as regards Biblical proof. Then there is "infant baptism" and "election" and you theologians only know how many more contested points of vital import to the whole.

The quest for a logical category of the Good and the Evil in the universe led Augusta and Mr. Harriss into a debate on the question: does Art transcend Nature "as far as the symbolizing of hidden truth, whether moral or intellectual?" As a devotee of Nature the young novelist could not take an entirely consistent stand. She says in defense of Art:

> Should not Excelsior be the watchword and motto of the true artist? Is not an artist a great reformer whose instructions are pictorial? To reform the world implies being above it, does it not?

Shakespeare is harshly condemned for his failure to

carry out the high moral obligations of the artist. She asks Mr. Harriss "what great Eternal truths" are incarnated in such characters as Hamlet, Othello, Iago, Macbeth, Shylock, Falstaff, and his Richards? Those who argue that these characters do present "Eternal truths" might just as well laud the moral values of *The Prince*—"though a darker web was never woven."

To clinch her argument on the potentialities of Art as a teacher of moral truths, Augusta expresses a conviction that became the greatest single factor in her literary career: "A great and good man's life well told is a work of art; that is, of the art I love. . . O! Art should elevate, should refine, should sanctify the heart." It is no exaggeration to say that the thousands of American readers who awaited expectantly each novel by Augusta Evans (readers generally innocent of Shakespeare's great non-theological truths) were influenced by the same critical standard which Miss Evans states here, namely, that Art's greatest function is to guide its followers toward the Gospel which Christ taught.

Even though Augusta's intellectual journey was a circuitous one, only bringing her back to the point from which she started, she achieved one goal which became the most vital interest of her life. She resolved to "combat scepticism to the day of my death, and if possible, to help others to avoid the thorny path I have trod ere I was convinced of the fallibility of human Reason." In this spirit she began the composition of *Beulah*, the novel which brought nation-wide acclaim to the youthful Mobilian.

The letters of Augusta to the scholarly minister are

couched in such emotional language, and contain so many personal allusions, that we cannot help wondering if her interest in him was prompted by romantic as well as ecclesiastical ties. In October of 1856 she wrote him: "My friend, what 'hindrance' should there be to our cheerful meeting? After two years of absence did you doubt your sister would welcome you to her country home? Ah Brother mine, I do trust your health may be restored . . ." Mr. Harriss was only four years older than Augusta and had been admitted into the Alabama Conference of the Methodist Episcopal Church South at the age of twenty-one. They probably met when he served as chaplain at the Navy Yard in 1853-1854. During the next ten years he held appointments at several small churches in south Alabama, and in 1864 he was superannuated because of poor health. He died in 1866, at a time when Augusta Evans's name was mentioned throughout the South for her great services to the cause which she valued more highly than her personal happiness.[32]

CHAPTER VI

Beulah: a Human Document in an Old Conflict

1859

THE IMPACT OF SCIENCE upon faith in the nineteenth century shook pillars of tradition in every area of experience. Today, it is difficult to gauge the alarm with which our grandparents viewed the dangers of "pure reason" and the "scientific method." They questioned the wisdom of doubting the ways and beliefs of their fathers, or of reasoning too closely upon them, especially since the gains of the re-examination showed little promise of compensating for many lost assurances and doubted certitudes. What proof did they have that the new crusader after truth was pursuing a righteous end, with the happiness of humanity as his goal, if he must strip himself of cherished conventions and enter battle with such cold weapons as objectivity, open-mindedness, and technical precision?

The question may sound academic today, but it was once viewed as a major conflict in everyday life, embracing deep convictions on the nature of evil. The issue was often correlated with a very simple scheme of psychology, in which the elements of goodness were ranged on the side of the *heart,* and elements of evil (of which doubt of religious principles ranked high) were associated with the *mind.* It is sometimes charged that our ancestors' defense of the warm, human affections in the name of religion, and their attack upon the impersonal, calculating forces of the mind as evil influences, were merely latter-day battles in the old war between the authority of *the word* and the validity of *free inquiry.* This is partly true, but intellectual Victorians, particularly those sharing the moral courage of Carlyle, Wordsworth, Arnold and Tennyson, saw deeper implications in the conflict. They feared the objectivity of the scientist as a potential danger to human relationships (and many people in this atomic age still share their fears). The forces of tradition and feeling, though crippling to the scientist's or to the logician's approach to truth, were foundations of strength in the scheme of values that were opposed to intellectual liberalism a century ago.

It is important to remember, however, that many a man of that earnest, "Reflective Age" could place himself on the side of the angels and yet agree with the Victorian poet:

> There lives more faith in honest doubt,
> Believe me, than in half the creeds.

It was a question of emphasis and of loss—of protecting areas of experience which were bound to suffer at the hands of objective investigators. As early as 1798

Wordsworth had rallied the forces who defended the *heart* with the stirring words:

One impulse from a vernal wood
May teach you more of man,
Of moral evil and of good,
Than all the sages can.

Sweet is the lore which Nature brings;
Our meddling intellect
Misshapes the beauteous forms of things:—
We murder to dissect.

Enough of Science and of Art;
Close up those barren leaves;
Come forth, and bring with you a heart
That watches and receives.

But Wordsworth's nature worship and pantheism were not the safest guides to the conventional Christian, even though this poet's reliance upon feeling and intuition had much in common with the evangelism that swept through Protestant sects during the nineteenth century. A later poet, Tennyson, came to an unassailable position, so far as argument is concerned, and his resolution of the problem of doubt is still widely quoted:

Strong Son of God, immortal Love,
    Whom we, that have not seen thy face,
    By faith, and faith alone, embrace,
Believing where we cannot prove.

To those who believed as he, and Augusta Evans was among them, no further evidence was needed, no analysis, no proof, because Truth is what we *know* in our hearts is true. Thus a new mysticism was born, nurtured with the impelling strangeness of the word *intuition*, a basis for belief that was rejected by probers who must rely upon evidence, verification, and reasoning. It was a welcome talisman to the masses of people who usually take sides with the democracy of feeling, particularly when opposed to the aristocracy of thought.

Many great minds of the period found artistic expression for the conflict of heart and head. It is noteworthy also that most of them were keenly aware of the dramatic possibilities of the problem, and they sought to project the issue into highly emotional narratives, essays and poems—*The Sorrows of Werther*, *Lyrical Ballads*, *Sartar Resartus*, *Walden*, *In Memoriam*, *The Scarlet Letter*, *Leaves of Grass*, and many more. Some of the authors' most exciting passages were generally accepted as personal experiences.

It is not surprising, then, to find an ambitious young woman down in Mobile, Alabama, one innocent of schools but steeped in erudition and sentimental fiction, who conceived the notion that thousands of readers awaited her first philosophical novel, a study of her own struggle to preserve her orthodox Methodism from the dangers of scepticism. *Beulah* will never be ranked with the great works of our language, but the popularity of this sincere narrative is a compliment to a reading public which could take its sentimentality with a dash of mental salt.

Miss Evans's fictional confession, with its appropriate Biblical title of *Beulah*, is a far more ambitious novel than her first romance, *Inez, a Tale of the Alamo*. The central problem in the work is the relationship between the heroine and Dr. Guy Hartwell. He sees that his passionate love is returned with only the affection of a girl for her guardian, and he goes away for five years, while Beulah studies, struggles with scepticism, performs numerous acts of charity, and publishes didactic literature. After 510 pages of anguish, zeal, and impressive erudition, Beulah is a Christian again, and Dr. Hartwell's opportune arrival from the Orient renews the weak love interest. The heroine not only accepts his proposal of marriage but consents to guide him into Heaven. The author takes it for granted that the girl's understanding of morality is superior to the man's—because of her womanly intuition—and she assumes that a wife's major duty in life is to see that her husband and children go to Heaven.

Much of Beulah's struggle with doubt runs parallel with Augusta Evans's, as seen in her letters to the Reverend Mr. Harriss, but the author takes greater pains in documenting the heroine's progress through speculation. In assigning the stages of Beulah's ordeal to certain books and authors, Miss Evans must have believed that she would render her readers a great service, morally and culturally.

It is a tribute to the intellectual curiosity of our ancestors that a popular book like *Beulah* should contain so many discussions of theology, philosophy, literature and science, through which the heroine plods in her search for a rational basis for her religious faith. She is launched on "the sea of Cosmogonies" by Poe's "Eureka," and before she is conscious of it, she is the victim of a "seemingly infallible reasoning" which, at the conclusion, coolly informs her that she is her own God. The philosophy of "this methodical madman" is pleasantly bewildering to Beulah. Later she is forced to admit that Poe's reasoning was "the portal through which she entered the vast Pantheon of Speculation."

After Poe, comes DeQuincey's *Analects from Richter,* a work which Beulah believes will become a guide to her soul, but suggestions of pre-existence and transmigration of souls baffle her, and the thought that her own soul, "chiliads old," has entered her body "fresh from the release of a hangman, instead of coming down on angel wings from its starry home," does not offer consolation for the Christian dogmas which it challenges.

The heroine's troubled quest for assurances and certitudes, on which to build a faith more acceptable to her reason than orthodox Christianity, leads her through Emerson, Carlyle, Goethe, Theodore Parker, more of Richter, Feurbach, Kant, and Coleridge. At one point she doubts "the plan of redemption as taught by divines, as laid down in the New Testament" and wonders if it is logical to "curse a race in order to necessitate a Savior." Transcendentalism charms her at first, but after a thorough course of reading, she dismisses German speculation as "ignes-fatui . . . 'confusion worse confounded.' " In desperation she kneels to pray, but she wonders to whom she is addressing her passionate supplications. To Nature? To Heroes? She throws "herself down to sleep with a shivering dread, as of a young child separated from its mother, wailing in some starless desert."

Fearful that orthodox Christians might misunderstand her, Miss Evans speaks out passionately in defense of a reverent love for nature:

> Alas for the besotted soul who cannot bend the knee of humble adoration before nature's altar, where sacrifices are offered to Jehovah, pavilioned in invisibility. There is an ardent love of nature as far removed from gross materialism or subtle pantheism on the one hand as from stupid inappreciation on the other. There is such a thing as looking "through nature up to nature's God," notwithstanding the frightened denials of those who, shocked at the growing materialism of the age, would fain persuade this generation to walk blindfold through the superb temple a loving God has placed us in.

Plodding with a desperate earnestness through the philosophies of modern times, finding none which satisfied her mind and her heart, Beulah is at the point of accepting Dr. Hartwell's conclusion, which is the "everlasting basis of all scepticism: there is no criterion of truth! All must be but subjectively, relatively true!" Her guardian advises her to give up the search for a completely rational explanation of creation, life and death. "Oh, child, do you not see how matters stand?" he argues. "Why, how can the finite soul cope with Infinite Being? . . . Pantheism or utter scepticism—there is no retreat." She comes upon Tennyson's *Palace of Art,* and the meaning she gets from it—"love of beauty and intellectual culture cannot satisfy the God-given aspirations of the soul"—is so contrary to her own educational standards that she publishes a refutation of the poem. Dr. Hartwell warns her that in her worship of the human mind, she has reared for herself a "palace [on] . . . dreary, inaccessible crags."

Undaunted, she tackles Locke, Descartes, Cousin,

Sidney Smith, Hume, William Hamilton, Spinoza, and the commentaries upon their works. The physical laws of the universe are questioned: "There is a broken cog somewhere in the machinery of this plunging globe of ours. Everything organic, or inorganic, bears testimony to a miserable derangement. There is not a department of earth where harmony reigns."

At last Beulah cries out wearily, in language almost identical with that used by Augusta in her letters to the minister: "Oh better die than live as I have lived, in perpetual strugglings! What is life worth without peace of mind, without hope." Eager to have the battle over, she seizes upon a rational argument that satisfied her previously uncompromising reason: her scepticism had forced her to reject "Christian theism because [she] could not understand how God had created the Universe out of nothing." And yet the same scepticism had embraced a premise equally confusing: that the "Universe created laws, that matter gradually created mind." Recognition of this inconsistency in her thinking leads her to the assumption that only God could be the First Mover of causes and the Creator of life. She humbles "her proud intellect," leaves the "icy shadow" of scepticism, and passes into the consoling haven of "the holy religion of Jesus Christ," where her "weary Spirit found rest . . . that rest which only the exhausted wanderer through the burning wastes of speculation can truly comprehend and appreciate." The author takes for granted that Beulah's needs are largely emotional, that her victory is the result of a cry of the *heart* against the tyranny of the *head*.

Miss Evans's analysis of Beulah's spiritual victory was unsatisfactory to several contemporaries, two of whom were her personal friends. Henry Timrod, the South Carolina poet who was soon to be called the "Laureate of the Confederacy," wrote Augusta's close friend, Rachel Lyons, that he was disappointed in the treatment of "the bold speculations" in *Beulah*. He had been led to expect a more artistic construction of this philosophical debate. "Beulah's transition from scepticism to Faith," he writes, "is left almost unaccounted for. How much I should like to have my own doubts settled in the same satisfactory, yet most inexplicable manner!"[33]

Rachel Lyons wrote Augusta about Timrod's objections and indicated that her aunt shared the poet's views. On October 17, 1859, Augusta answered this criticism in language that every orthodox Methodist of the time would approve. She thanked her friend warmly for reporting this objection to the structure of her novel: "Verily, there are numbers to flatter me, but very few, sufficiently my friends, to tell me honestly of my faults." Augusta argues:

> The truth of the whole matter lies in a nut-shell—our religious states are determined by *Faith, not Reason*. The preponderance of the Rationalistic element in Beulah's organization necessitated her speculative career; she searched all creeds and systems, rejected all, because in all she found inscrutable mysteries which reason could not pierce and elucidate; consequently she trembled on the very confines of pyrrhonism (you must pardon the *seeming* pedantry implied in the use of this term, for all sciences have their necessary and peculiar phraseology). Beulah constituted her Reason the sole criterion of truth, but found on all sides insolvable mys-

teries—found that unaided by that Revelation which her reason had ignored that she was utterly incapable of ever arriving at any belief. She found that erudition and tireless research availed nothing; that without Divine aid, Man as Man was too finite to cope with the secrets of the Universe, to solve the great questions of God! Eternity! Destiny! and discarding the belief that Reason alone could discover the truth, she rested her spent soul in the Ark of Faith! whereby she was enabled to receive the sublime teachings of *Inspiration.*

Augusta explains that her purpose in developing Beulah's ordeal with scepticism is "to prove the fallacy of all human, philosophical systems, the limited nature of human faculties, the total insufficiency of our reason to grapple with the vital questions which are propounded by every earnest mind." She believes that all honest doubters will inevitably fall back upon "the absolute necessity of trusting in the revelations of Jehovah! the Great I Am!" Asking pardon of her friend who was of orthodox Hebrew faith, she adds that "our blessed Lord Jesus Christ" must also be accepted. She concludes her defense of Beulah's victory with these words, "Because Beulah trusted to Rationalism, she was wretched and sceptical; but when she put faith in the word of the Living God, she found 'the ways of pleasantness and the paths of peace.' "

Three years after the publication of *Beulah,* Augusta was questioned on the propriety of the philosophical debate in the novel. She assumes that her friend, Miss Janie Tyler of Richmond, Virginia, sees an unfeminine quality in such probings into questions of doubt and faith. In answer to Miss Tyler's statement that metaphysics must be the novelist's "passion," Augusta writes,

"I could smile at your estimate of me, if I were not aware that you predicated it from a by-no-means uncommon error that an author's mental or moral idiosyncrasies are clearly indexed in his or her books. Pardon me if I insist that this is an unsafe criterion." She cites the varied interests of several authors and then gives her reasons for analyzing the problem of fundamentalism versus speculation in *Beulah*: "Because a grim and goading scepticism forced an earnest soul to grapple with the arcana of metaphysics in the hope of attaining the absolutely true, is it just or logical to conclude that her aesthetic sensibilities are necessarily blunted? Nay, is it not rather the contrary, that as Cousin contends, 'the true, good and beautiful' are inseparably bound up? Judged by the canons of Feudal ages, woman's desire for logical certitude in her beliefs might well be termed 'unfeminine'; but the criteria of the nineteenth century claim to be more exalted, and we hold that to be 'feminine' is scarcely a synonym for weak-minded, idiotic, or frivolous. If I have given much time and attention to the abstruse speculations of metaphysicians, it was because I feared their ethical creed was insidious and deleterious to earnest, unsettled young thinkers, and I strove to combat their arguments for love of my countrymen and women, rather than through fondness for their vexed and tortuous paths."[34]

The struggle between speculation and fundamentalism in Beulah's mind is not the only portion of this serious book which she hoped would "do good." Numerous passages remind the reader of his sacred duties with regard to home, friends, church, the under-privileged, and government. Such sermons as the following are not needed in the action of *Beulah,* but they contribute greatly to the author's major purpose:

Oh, woman! woman! when will you sever the fetters which fashion, wealth and worldliness have bound about you, and prove yourselves worthy of the noble mission for which you were created? How much longer will heartless, soulless wives, mothers, daughters, and sisters, waltz, moth-like, round the consuming flame of fashion; and by neglecting their duties, and deserting their sphere, drive their husbands, sons and brothers, out into the world, reckless and depraved. . . God help the women of America! . . . Teach them that gilded saloons, with their accompanying allurements of French latitude of conversation . . . tend to the depths of social evil; and oh, lead them back to the hearthstone, that holy-post, which too many, alas, have deserted.

CHAPTER VII

A Celebrity

1859-1860

EARLY IN THE SUMMER of 1859 Augusta left her home in Summerville, a suburb of Mobile, to which the family had moved a year before, and traveled to New York in the company of her cousin, Colonel John W. Jones of Columbus, Georgia, for the purpose of selling her novel. The manuscript had been mailed to Appleton before their departure, and soon after their arrival in New York, this publisher returned the novel to their hotel with a brief note of rejection. The persistent couple then called upon J. C. Derby, of the firm of Derby and Jackson, who had published successful novels by rival sentimentalists, particularly "Marion Harland" (Mary Virginia Terhune) and Miriam Coles Harris. In his memoirs Derby describes the visit of the "young lady of pleasant address and marked intelligence" and her cousin, "a fiery young Southerner."[35] The publisher was impressed by Augusta's brusque honesty, especially her admission that the sale of her first novel "was not very encouraging" and that the present work had been rejected by Appleton. He agreed to submit the manuscript to the judgment of his own family—a shrewd decision which aptly

Augusta Jane Evans in 1865

Augusta's Mother, Sarah Howard Evans

illustrates Derby's awareness of the tastes to which the novel was addressed.

In recounting his next interview with Miss Evans and her cousin, Derby mentions an amusing incident which he implies was characteristic of the zeal and impulsiveness of these young Southerners. While the publisher kept them in suspense with his questions, Colonel Jones pretended to examine the books on the shelves of the office, but in reality (as he later confessed) he was preparing to hurl a book at Derby's head when the expected rejection was announced. This violent demonstration of loyalty was pleasantly averted when the publisher informed them that his family had decided unanimously that *Beulah* must be issued at once. Derby concludes, "Colonel Jones was a most estimable man, devotedly attached to his cousin. [Four years later] he fell at the sanguinary battle of Gettysburg, fighting for the cause which both of them believed to be sacred."

On her return to Mobile later in the summer, Miss Evans seems to have interested herself mainly in the controversy over slavery and its accompanying questions of regional sovereignty. She was undoubtedly influenced by her trip to the North, where she became familiar with the recent progress of revolutionary aspects of Abolition. She witnessed Northern acquiescence in the violent proposals of John Brown, who was ready to arm slaves so that they might kill their masters. She heard newly converted Republicans defend Hinton Helper's plan to tax slavery out of existence. Her experiences convinced her that the time had come for loyal Southerners to meet "the impending crisis," as Helper characterized the issue.[36] Augusta decided to level her own attack against an area of Northern culture, the region's literature and journalism, which many Americans in every section had accepted as the best and most idealistic product of our civilization. This plan was shrewd propaganda, no matter what one may think of its historical and critical accuracy. Perhaps she had learned good lessons from the clever propagandists of Abolition—Mrs. Stowe, Garrison, Whittier, even Lincoln.

Augusta Evans is certainly the author of a series of articles which appeared in the Mobile *Daily Advertiser* in October and November of 1859, unsigned but admittedly by the same author.[37] The clever rhetoric of these pieces not only contains ideas often expressed in her novels, but the articles are written in a style distinctly like her own—a style unlike that of any contemporary Mobile author or journalist.[38]

The first two articles appear under the heading "Northern Literature" and their two companion-pieces under "Southern Literature." Their arguments present a subtle brand of counter-propaganda to the oft repeated charge that the South must accept responsibility for sanctioning an immoral institution. Instead of defending slavery, this author hurls charges of immorality against writers who publish in the land of "Black Republicanism" and against the audience which accepts their lies and indecencies in the name of culture. Sensational writing of this calibre always sells well, she argues, and since the dollar is all that matters up there,

Northern readers assume that its literary value is high. The outpouring of Northern presses is something less than a national asset, as often claimed; it is "a disgrace to its authors and insulting to the intelligence of the American people." Southern readers are assured that noble literature has no political axe to grind, and that the propaganda machines of the North may be dismissed as unsound in principle and suspect in motive. She charges that Northern literature neglects its moral duty to instruct in order that it may cater to popular taste and earn money; thus its appeal is to the basest instincts of man, and its influence fosters immorality.

No clearer indication is needed that the time is ripe for war than abuse of this kind, leveled at a region's belles-lettres, which are nonpartisan for the most part. The acceptance of a *de facto* division between the North and South in 1859, the emotional tenor of the style, and the stress upon what were conceived to be "principles" rather than party or regional policies, suggest that the author was dedicated to the views of another widely advertised States Rights advocate from Alabama—William Lowndes Yancey—whose persuasive oratory in support of the Southern position had already led thousands of Alabamians far along the road of rebellion against the rising tide of Abolition.

One recognizes in Miss Evans's argument (if it is hers) the hate symbols commonly urged against the North at the time, and conversely, the implied opposites which were soon to find cherished places in the South's view of its cause: (1) Northerners are cold and mercenary (Southerners are genial and idealistic); (2) love of money has made Northerners corrupt and impersonal (Southerners prefer refined, humanitarian sentiment to material forms of wealth); (3) literature in the North is viewed objectively as a commercial product (Southerners write from their hearts, with beauty and truth as their aims); and (4) Northerners debase literature for political ends (Southerners cherish the cultural, non-partisan values of literature). If judged solely as *propaganda,* these arguments were wisely chosen as instruments against such effective weapons in the cold war of 1840-1860 as *Uncle Tom's Cabin,* the speeches of Webster, Lincoln, and Garrison, and the poetry of Lowell and Whittier—all widely reprinted. The Mobilian's earliest rhetoric did not receive widespread distribution, but she was learning her craft so well that five years later the appeal of her *Macaria* forced a Northern general to issue a ban against the novel among his troops and to burn all available copies.[39]

In the fall of 1859 Augusta returned to New York with her uncle, Augustus Howard; they were house guests of the Derbys at their estate called Glenwood, after spending a few days at the St. Nicholas Hotel. The Mobile *Daily Advertiser* for September 18, 1859, noticed the event in this manner:

SOUTHERN FEMALE AUTHOR IN NEW YORK

The New York correspondent of the Charleston *Mercury* writes: "The stately and beautiful Miss Evans of Mobile . . . one of the most gifted daughters of the South, is now in this city, supervising the publication of a new novel. It will treat of American fashionable life from a Southern standpoint, and I predict, will reflect great credit on the charming authoress and add much to the literary stature of the South. Her receptions at the St. Nicholas are very brilliant.

Derby's printers were ready with their galley proofs when she arrived. The excited authoress spent her mornings with the pleasant chore of reading proof, and afternoons and evenings among the literary crowd which gathered at the publisher's house. It was during this visit that she met Miss Rachel Lyons of Columbia, South Carolina, a witty and beautiful debutante, who remained Augusta's closest friend for many years. Several years later Miss Lyons was courted by one of the most graceful lyricists of the Old South, Henry Timrod, who addressed at least one poem to her, "La Belle Juive," and described his personal sorrows to her in twenty or more love letters.[40] However, Rachel Lyons was indebted to Augusta Evans for the introduction to the man she later married, Dr. J. F. Heustis, a young physician of Mobile. The poet Timrod found a new love in the English girl, Katie Goodwin.

During this second visit to New York, a trivial incident occurred which Augusta often repeated with great amusement. Her dignified uncle Augustus secured tickets to a modern play, not knowing that a highlight of the performance was a ballet number. Stage dancing, particularly in the sparse costume of the ballet, was a questionable form of amusement to provincial Americans at that time, and when her uncle saw the exposed limbs of the dancers, he nudged his niece and murmured his shocked disapproval, "Don't look at the hussies." Gentleman that he was, Uncle Augustus looked into his lap, and Augusta did likewise. Such feelings as these unsophisticated people had on this occasion give us a clue to certain contemporary prejudices which affected many passages in Augusta's novels, though she was far more emancipated in her views of the arts than were thousands of her readers.

Augusta's visit with the Derbys was prolonged until the appearance of *Beulah.* Perhaps the most favorable early notice of the book was that which appeared in the New York Morning *Courier and Enquirer* on October 1, 1859. It was written by James Reed Spaulding, a pious young editor who believed that metropolitan journalism and American fiction would be healthier if their writers were more conscious of the principles of Christianity. Derby writes that Spaulding "became so much interested after reading [*Beulah*] that he called personally to learn the address of the author."[41] When Miss Evans and Spaulding later met at Derby's house, the scholarly couple were immediately attracted to each other. Before she left New York, Augusta agreed that the yankee journalist might visit Mobile to meet her parents and let them see if he would make a suitable son-in-law.

The fall, winter, and spring of 1859-1860 were probably the most exciting period of Augusta's life up to this time. She returned to Mobile with the news of her triumphs in New York: her prominent new friends, the publication of *Beulah,* the favorable reviews, her ardent suitor. The early sales of the novel surprised even its author, for 22,000 copies were printed in the first nine months, almost a best seller for those times.[42]

Royalty checks of substantial size would soon be in the mails, and in anticipation of them, Augusta was able to secure comforts for the family which bad luck and ill health had prevented her father from supplying. She laid plans to purchase the attractive house in Summerville, called "Georgia Cottage," in which they had been living for over a year.[43] Invitations to Miss Lyons and Mr. Spaulding were renewed and urged, and in preparation for their visits, Augusta redecorated the cottage and planted bulbs, ferns, and flowering shrubs on the expansive grounds, many of which are still blooming at Georgia Cottage in our time. Her domestic responsibilities, always assumed without complaint, were increased in May of 1860 when she undertook the important task of tutoring two of her sisters, Carrie and Sarah. She wrote Rachel that she was concentrating upon history and philosophy, using "Grote's Greece" and a translation of the *Iliad* for textbooks in history.[44]

Augusta and Rachel interchanged enthusiastic letters about their plans for the spring and summer. In January, Augusta urged her friend to consider a European tour with her: "Just fancy us both, safely landed in Rome; once there we could place ourselves under the protection of Elizabeth Barrett Browning, and her scarcely less illustrious Lord, Robert. Or if you did not particularly affect the 'poets of Parnassus' we could doubtless prevail on Charlotte Cushman or Harriet Hosmer to chaperone us."

These two young women (Augusta was then twenty-three years old and Rachel was twenty) were probably exceptional for their times, but a modern reader is astonished to see the mixture of girlish small-talk with learned commentaries on death in their letters: "Ah, how the Titans of this century are falling away," Augusta laments, "sinking from the crested wave of Time, into the vast, echoless depths of Eternity. In one brief year [1859-1860] how many glory-crowned heads have been placed beneath monumental marble: Comte, Sir William Hamilton, Prescott, Irving, Humboldt, DeQuincy, Leigh Hunt, and Macaulay." And she quotes fitting lines from Charles Lamb and Robert Southey on the passing of "old familiar faces."[45]

In February of 1860 Rachel wrote that their mutual friend, Dr. Caldwell, was slowly dying, and Augusta responded in these solemn and self-conscious tones: "Sometimes I smile when I find my heart bowing down before earthly idols, tightening the chain that binds it to dust. It seems to me that this is the unsolved problem, viz: to enjoy life, to be cheerful and happy, and yet remember constantly, that this is but a probationary state; that Earth is merely a vast vineyard in which the Father has laid out *work* for all of us. . . Oh dear Rachel! may you and I hold up rich purple clusters, as the fruit of our toil, when the Gathering Time rolls round."

Augusta constantly urged her friend to write a serious book: "Rachel write a Jewish tale; and make it a substratum on which to embroider your views of life, men, women, Art, Literature. . . Your surroundings and education have familiarized you with all the mystic points of your creed, and you might weave a tale of marvelous power."[46] A month later she continued reprovingly, "You admit that you are restless and dissatisfied with the weary round of fashion and gayety. Oh, my friend: no *true* woman ever yet fed contentedly on these husks. Our hearts are shrines for holier idols than the world can erect; they must have either Love or Duty. The fortunate and happiest women have both," but since Rachel does not plan to marry soon—and Augusta considered marriage a superior duty to authorship—she is advised to accomplish as much good as possible through writing. She must be warned, however, that it is her duty to "select the *very highest types* of character, for the standard has sadly deteriorated of late in works of fiction. In a too close imitation of *Nature,* many of our novelists have fallen into the error of patronizing coarseness, vulgarity, and ignorance." She cites *Adam Bede* as an example of coarse realism.

Rachel visited Georgia Cottage in the summer of 1860, and Augusta introduced her to Dr. Heustis. Three years later Augusta was able to give wise counsel to this pair of lovers whose courtship was hampered by such obstacles as difference in religion, residence six hundred miles apart, and a civil war. Apparently Rachel had "laughed at the idea that he could interest [her]" and had assured Augusta that she "could never marry a man like Dr. Heustis." So when Rachel finally admitted to Augusta that she loved Dr. Heustis, Augusta wrote her a stern letter in which she admonished her younger friend for ever being in doubt about Dr. Heustis's noble character and his sincere love for her. She adds, "To be candid with you, my dear Rachel, I must tell you that I was very much astonished to find from your letter that you had not informed your parents of your engagement. Oh Rachel! You owe it to them to acquaint them immediately with the solemn step you have taken, and the holy relationship which you occupy to Dr. Heustis." Augusta argues that Rachel's parents will offer no serious objection to Dr. Heustis's Christian faith.[47] Such wise advice apparently had its effect, for Rachel and Dr. J. F. Heustis were married on February 4, 1865.

James Reed Spaulding's visit to Mobile had to be postponed temporarily. Throughout the spring of 1860 he was busy with a scheme which would fulfill a life-long ambition: the founding of a newspaper with an editorial policy dedicated to the proposition that "the time has come for living Christianity to assert itself in secular journalism."[48] Funds for this enterprise were raised from members of various religious denominations, and on June 9, 1860, Spaulding's New York *World* issued its "Prospectus," informing its readers that its policy would be non-partisan politically, but admitting frankly that "in all its judgments upon the practical affairs of life" it will recognize "the authority and efficacy of Christian principles," though never "assuming or seeking to be a preacher of religious doctrine." Indicative of its tolerance in Christian ethics, the *World's* first issue (June 14, 1860) carried a reasonably unbiased summary of Darwin's *On the Origin of Species by Means of Natural Selection,* a work which appeared less than a year earlier and was already becoming the most controversial book of the century. The reviewer, probably Spaulding, admits the "rare fascination" of Darwin's views, but questions much of his scientific evidence, particularly the basic assumption of "survival of the fittest," pointing out that in some cases the "weakest" appear to have dominated.

Before the *World* was many issues old, James Spaulding visited Mobile and requested Augusta's hand in marriage. Tradition in the family persists that Spaulding made a splendid impression upon Augusta's parents and friends, in spite of his yankee birth and sympathies. Perhaps if the national strife about slavery and secession had not developed so swiftly in the next few months, this earnest young couple might have found some means of resolving their conflicting views on the great issue of the day, a difference which soon separated them irretrievably.

However, during the weeks preceding the excitement of Lincoln's nomination and campaign, Augusta found great happiness in her love for Spaulding. In addition, favorable reviews of *Beulah* continued to appear, each complimenting the great moral worth of this novel. *DeBow's Review,* a widely read journal, gave lavish praise to this work of "a young lady of Mobile, of charming address, manners, and conversation," who with "great sprightliness as well as depth of intellect," has produced "what may be considered one of the best American novels."[49] Another journal which was highly respected in the Evans household, *The Methodist Quarterly Review,* compared her writing favorably with that of George Eliot.[50] Generous praise came from a rival in sentimental fiction, Marion Harland, who said, "I pronounce it the best work of fiction ever published by a Southern writer . . . No American authoress has ever published a greater book."[51] The eminent *Southern Literary Messenger,* anticipating Miss Evans's regional prejudices of a few months later, devoted nine pages to an argument that books like *Beulah* indicate that Southern authors are destined to excel their Northern rivals because "the mind takes its impress from the scenes which surround it," and the South can offer its creative artists "the fairest forms of noble beauty," a valuable system of aesthetics, and a regional "fancy that culls the fairest flowers that bloom in the realms of ideal thought."[52]

There were a few unfavorable reviews, such as that which appeared in the Baltimore *Daily Exchange,* September 27, 1859, written by the reader who had rejected the manuscript for Appleton.[53] This critic calls *Beulah* a "very humble and feeble and intellectually unremunerative" imitation of *Jane Eyre.* He concludes that the novel "may sell but we cannot suppose its destiny is to be read—certainly it will never be admired or prized by competent judges." He apologizes for attacking the work of a woman so vigorously, and he "sincerely trusts that she does not write for subsistence, as we cannot hope that she will make it this way—for *Beulah* presents no indication that the writer is capable of better things." This diatribe (Derby sent Augusta a copy of it), conceived petulantly by one who was attempting to justify his previous verdict on the book's bad prospects for public acceptance, must have given Augusta and her friends much amusement in the years when her novels were sold, read and discussed throughout the land.

Perhaps the review which pleased the author most was one which Spaulding ran in the sixth issue of the *World* (June 20, 1860), written undoubtedly by Augusta's suitor. The success of *Beulah,* the critic argues, "is an encouraging indication of public taste." He praises the handling of Beulah's struggle with doubt and concludes that Miss Evans is an exception among women, one gifted not only with the purest of feminine traits, but endowed with a capacity to handle metaphysics. In the light of Spaulding's personal interest in the author, the whimsical turn which he gives the conclusion of this review reads like a public acknowledgment of his intentions. He objects to the author's stress upon the sternness of males and upon the vigor with which the heroine resists the advances of her suitor. "We trust that our author has made her Beulah a *little too strong,*" he concedes. "But for the encouragement of our sex, of whom, let us hope, there are some worthy to mate with such spirits as Beulah, we indulge the trust that they will not prove as obdurate against an honest suit as she—except in fiction."

Spaulding's visit to Mobile was made within a few weeks of the publication of this review. At first there was no "obduracy" against his "honest suit," but he did not reckon with the young lady's "strong" will—one that could apply itself as tenaciously to regional patriotism, and against those who opposed the South, as it did in *Beulah* to the pursuit of an acceptable religious faith.

Augusta and James Spaulding had much in common, in spite of their political views. Both were idealists with the zeal of reformers, and neither had much patience with compromises. Their mutual friend, J. C. Derby, described Spaulding as "a grave, taciturn man, of large frame and powerful intellect." A few years later Spaulding became "the boldest master of political invective ever known on the American press," Derby thought. He was a man of "great soul and honest purpose."[54]

The impressions which Augusta Evans made upon interviewers at about this time (1860), in her twenty-fourth year, suggest that her temperament was as serious, earnest and thoughtful as Spaulding's. In appearance, she was slim and willowy, with masses of brown hair. Her best feature was a broad, graceful forehead. Her eyes were unusually alert, but her expression was so prevailingly serious that her eyes appeared to be sharp rather than brilliant. Again, thoughtfulness was probably responsible for the set of her mouth and chin, which several people described as firm and determined. Everyone commented upon her sprightly conversation, and after the publication of such erudite works as *Beulah* and *St. Elmo,* interviewers were delighted to observe that her spoken language had no kinship with the speech which her heroes and heroines often affected. Several people mentioned the soft, musical quality of her voice, and almost every record of her character emphasizes the dignity and charm of her manners. She was never described as a beautiful woman—as were her companions, Misses Rachel Lyons and Frank Crawford—but no one ever called her plain. A lively temperament and obvious sincerity more than made up for the beauty that she might have lacked.

There was a quality in Augusta's character which some people of our time will condemn as imperious or haughty, but it is doubtful that many of her readers would have understood our meaning. In choosing between right and wrong in conduct or belief, she *was* stern, uncompromising. But we must remember that her approach to moral and ethical questions was Victorian. She believed that the right course or the good thing is readily identified, that its quality of goodness never alters, and she firmly opposed the view that "conditions" alter rules or standards. The latter frame of mind she condemned as weak, unstable. And like a few of the intellectual giants of her time, she associated the "open mind" with the dangers that are certain to follow when people reject tradition in favor of progress. Under provocation, Augusta was imperious, but her followers saw a majesty in her position, not an arrogance, and they felt more secure as she reminded them of the rules of life which they had learned at their mothers' firesides.

CHAPTER VIII

Propagandist and War Nurse

1860-1863

SOMETIME during the last months of 1860 Augusta Evans decided that her love for James Spaulding was not compatible with her love for the South, and she terminated their engagement. The correspondence between the two does not survive, but we can trace aspects of their conflicting loyalties by examining their published views upon "the impending crisis" at the time of their decision against marriage.

The issues of the New York *World* for the weeks immediately preceding the national election of 1860 reveal Spaulding's uneasiness over the South's threats of reprisal in the event of Lincoln's success. On October 17 an editorial demands calm judgment, patience and tolerance for the views and leadership of the Republican nominee. The writer reminds Lincoln's opponents, particularly those in the South, that his success at the polls will not mean destruction of the South, that Lincoln will be very circumspect in his treatment of the slavery question, because he will want to prove that the apprehensions of the South have been false.

Two days later Spaulding quotes excerpts from Southern papers which caution their readers against

Georgia Cottage As It Looks Today

St. Elmo As It Looks Today

Rachel Lyons Heustis

Henry Timrod

precipitant action. Among them is an editorial from the Mobile *Register,* which warns against "trifling" and "childish" conduct in the event of Lincoln's election—conduct which might deprive the city of useful Federal services. Spaulding praises this calm position and offers a reminder, on the same editorial page, that one of the leaders of the secession movement, Barnwell Rhett of South Carolina, has just been defeated by a representative Southern electorate. He interprets this as a sign that opposition to Abolition does not necessarily mean support of disunion.

As the national situation became more intense, and talk of civil war was heard on every hand, Spaulding ran an editorial (October 23, 1860) with a strangely prophetic message to his Southern friends: a war against the North cannot be won by the South, he argues, because the South does not grow enough foodstuffs to feed itself during a long campaign! A week later, in the issue of October 31, the tone of the *World's* editorial page is somewhat harsher. To Southerners who threaten secession after Lincoln's election, Spaulding says, "With the first overt act of treason, the heavy hand of the executive will fall; and those who once feel its weight will hardly need a second lesson."

After the election, the *World* had no compromise to offer the South and consistently urged the North to back the new President's policies. Such loyalty to Lincoln and to the Union was received by ardent States Righters as *prima facie* evidence of complete opposition to the Southern cause. In the light of Augusta Evans's zealous defense of the Southern position in 1860 and

1861, there is little wonder that her affections cooled toward the yankee journalist.

During the heat of the controversy over secession (January, 1861), Augusta received a letter from Mrs. L. Virginia French requesting that she add her name to a "Memorial" which would be presented to the Georgia Convention in an effort to forestall the secession of Georgia. Miss Evans wrote a stinging rebuke to the Tennessee authoress:

> . . . You will, I trust, pardon me when candor compels the avowal that with such a memorial I have no sympathy whatever . . . You have warmly espoused the "Union" cause, while I am an earnest and uncompromising Secessionist. . . Prompt and separate state action I believe to be the only door of escape from the worse than Egyptian bondage of Black Republicanism. For fifteen years, we of the South have endured insult and aggression; have ironed down our just indignation, and suffered numberless encroachments, because of our devotion to the "Union"; because we shuddered and shrank from laying hands on the magnificent Temple which our forefathers reared in proud triumph. . . Presuming upon their devotion, Northern fanaticism has grown on Southern endurance, and not all the diplomacy, the consummate statesmanship of patriotic men of both sections has weighed one iota against the waves of Abolitionism, which have rolled rapidly on till they threaten to pollute the sacred precincts of the White House. The "Union" has become a misnomer, and rather than witness the desecration of our glorious Fane, we of the South will Sampson-like lay hold upon its pillars, and if need be, perish in its ruins.[55]

She continues with a vigorous attack upon the "unscrupulous character" of the Republican leaders, who would inveigle the South into some kind of compromise, only to violate it later and thus destroy the

South. As her argument progresses, the emotional tenor of her letter becomes more intense:

> I repeat it: the Union has been an idol too long to admit of its being struck rudely from its lofty pedestal without sending a thrill of anguish to every true, patriotic heart; but my dear Madam, the law of *self-preservation* is imperative; and as the thirteen States cut the chains of Great Britain to regain their birthright, Freedom, so we of the South sever the galling links that bind us to a people who guided by the Demon of Fanaticism have insanely destroyed the noblest government which the accumulated wisdom of centuries has ever erected. . . It is because I most earnestly deprecate as *suicidal* an effort to delay the dissolution of the Union, that I must decline to add my own signature [to the memorial].

In the light of Lincoln's views on the South, she believes that armed conflict in support of the Southern position is inevitable, and she regards it "as an *economy of blood* for the fifteen States to secede as promptly as possible." She is proud to announce that Alabama has "irrevocably linked [her] destiny with the Carolinas," and like other Alabamians who are ready to "drain [their] veins rather than yield to the ignominious rule of Black Republicanism," she will support the Confederacy to the end.

The uncompromising quality of Augusta Evans's Southernism is expressed in most of her letters of this time, particularly in those passages which dismiss prominent women from her circle of friends because they now support the Union. Of Mrs. Mary Virginia Terhune, a rival in sentimental fiction who used the penname of "Marion Harland," she wrote in 1862:

> It was with painful emotions of mingled shame and indignation

that I learned that "Marion Harland," the boast and ornament of Virginia literature, had deserted the cause of her native state, of the bleeding South, who had felt so proud of her genius . . . [and] remained at the North, living contentedly among the oppressors of the *only free* people left upon the American continent. I have been told her husband voted for Lincoln; but I am amazed that she ever for one instant suffered his abolition views to distort and discolor her own. I met her in New York whither she came from her parsonage at Newark to see me, and I confess I was fascinated by a sort of "bonhomie," indescribable but irresistible. She impressed me as a genial, impulsive, noble-souled, warm-hearted Southern woman, par excellence, and I am totally unprepared for the announcement that she remained at the North, siding with the Philistines at this great crisis. I am mortified that a Southern woman should thus disgrace her section.[56]

Augusta was particularly worried about the political views of Mrs. Almira Hart Phelps, author of textbooks and principal of the famous Patapsco Female Institute near Baltimore. She told Miss Janie Tyler (a Richmond authoress and alumna of Patapsco) that when Beauregard "redeems his sacred promise to plant the Battle Flag of our Confederacy on the time-honored square of the Monumental City," she hoped to "have the privilege of clasping the hand of [Mrs. Phelps] whose past history claims my warmest admiration and to whom the youth of our country are under incalcuable obligations," but if this famous educator espouses the cause of Lincoln, as do many Marylanders, "the painful revelation that she sympathized with the unscrupulous wretches who are invading Southern soil would strike her rudely from the lofty pedestal where

I long ago placed her." She begs Miss Tyler to inquire about Mrs. Phelps's political views.[57]

Such comments explain the barrier which politics placed between Augusta Evans and the editor of the New York *World*. James Spaulding's zeal for the Union remained undiminished throughout the war, and in all the South there was no more ardent Confederate than Augusta Jane Evans.

It is unlikely that Augusta met Spaulding again after 1860 or renewed her correspondence with him. The editor was stricken with paralysis in the late sixties, and died in 1872.[58]

The exciting events of February, 1861, when Jefferson Davis was forming a new government in Montgomery, fascinated the youthful authoress, and she hurried to the capital to witness the memorable sessions. The regard with which she was held by Southern leaders is evident in the brief record of her visit. Thomas Cobb, a delegate from Georgia, wrote his wife on February 26 that he had met the celebrated novelist from Mobile: "A friend came to me this morning and said that a lady on the other side of the hall was anxious to make my acquaintance. Of course I assented and found that it was Miss Evans, the author of *Beulah*. She is very young-looking, though not pretty and very loquacious and sensible."[59] Two days later Cobb mentioned her again: "Mr. Hilliard invited me to a tea-drinking at his house tomorrow to meet Miss Evans."[60] Next to William Lowndes Yancey, Henry W. Hilliard was probably the most widely quoted politician in Alabama. He had been a professor at the University and a congressman, but was best known for his debates against secession. At the time he entertained Miss Evans, he was undoubtedly in search of a face-saving excuse to announce his espousal of the Confederacy. Lincoln's call for volunteers, a few weeks later, offered Hilliard a pretext for accepting a commission in the Confederate army.[61]

Soon after her return to Mobile, Augusta began to serve the new nation as fully as a woman was permitted to do at that time. Sandbags were urgently needed for the ramparts at Fort Morgan, where her father and two of her brothers, Howard and Vivian, were serving as volunteers. Augusta organized a corps of Mobile women to do the sewing, and within a few days nine thousand bags were ready for the garrison at the fort.

On January 22, 1862, she wrote Rachel that she had just returned from a visit to Fort Morgan, where she delivered a speech to the "Beulah Guards." She enclosed a copy of the speech and comments proudly, "You will see that I have inaugurated the *black flag* on our coast," apparently a reference to a suggestion that Federal coastal shipping be seized as prizes of war.

A camp for the training of troops was established near Georgia Cottage in 1861, and Augusta observed that illness was very common among the soldiers. Army medical corps at that time were not equipped to supply competent nurses for all bed-ridden cases. Miss Evans's reputation as a volunteer nurse was widely known in Mobile, and when she proposed that an army hospital be established in a vacant house near her home, where she and her friends could assist the doctors, the local

Commandant accepted the offer immediately. The hospital was officially named "Camp Beulah," in honor of her last novel.[62] In January of 1862 Augusta described her work at the hospital to a young friend in Virginia:

> For two months past I have been constantly engaged in nursing sick soldiers, keeping sleepless vigil by day and night, and this morning sitting beside one whose life has hung upon a slender thread for many days. My hand glides to his feeble pulse even while I write . . . Many times since I began this [letter] I have laid down my pen to administer medicine, count pulse, dress blisters, and perform many offices which absent sisters and mothers would gladly relieve me of if they could only be with their dear ones. God bless our noble army, and preserve them from the pestilence and suffering which have decimated their ranks during the past few months.[63]

Not long after this she gave General Beauregard a dramatic account of one experience at Camp Beulah: ". . . Three days ago, I was sitting beside a sick soldier, who was entirely delirious with fever. Suddenly, opening his eyes, he grasped my hand, and asked eagerly, 'Did you say General Beauregard was on Arlington Heights?' I answered, 'Be quiet, and go to sleep; *he will be there, very soon.*' "[64]

In March of 1862 Augusta expected to be called to areas nearer the battlefields. She wrote Miss Janie Tyler that she was "very busy making all necessary arrangements to enable me to leave home at any moment when I am notified that my services are needed elsewhere."[65] Battles would soon take place in Tennessee and Mississippi, she adds, and "we are organizing a corps of nurses for the hospital now in course of erection. I have determined to devote myself to the duties of the hospital." However, she did not accept this call, but remained in

Mobile, nursing at Camp Beulah and planning a wartime novel which would probably serve the cause more effectively than nursing at the battlefields.

All of her energies were thrown into the war effort. She wrote Miss Tyler, "The present crisis is so replete with interest, the questions involved so vital, the ties that link us as a people so inexpressibly dear, that I find no leisure for my studies, have neither inclination nor time to sit, as formerly over my desk, and give myself up unreservedly to communion with the grand old master-thinkers—the noble souls entombed in the glorious volumes of my library. While a nation's history is daily being written, page by page, in characters of blood, one has little thought for the dusty records of the dim bygone."[66]

She quickly became a studious critic of public affairs. On October 3, 1861, she wrote Rachel Lyons of her disappointment in the hesitant policies of the Confederate administration, which would not permit the victorious army at Manassas to pursue the "demoralized and panic-stricken" Federal troops to Washington, where "terms of peace" should have been written by the light of the flaming city. "The inexplicable policy of the Richmond Cabinet," she continues, "the evident timidity of President Davis . . . and the disgraceful conduct of affairs in Western Virginia all tend to impress me with the melancholy apprehension that the war will 'drag its slow length along,' possibly for years. . . "She was "haunted by the fear that *our leaders lack nerve.*"

In Augusta's long letters to J. L. M. Curry, influential congressman from Alabama before 1861 and Confederate congressman and colonel during the war, several significant political issues are argued so forcefully and intelligently that one can understand why prominent men like Curry, Henry Hilliard, Benjamin Hill, General Beauregard, and Robert Toombs listened closely to her counsel. She sternly opposed the infamous Exemption Bill, which enabled many wealthy Confederates to escape conscription. In her argument she exposes a grave weakness in the legislative processes of the Confederacy: *secret debate* on such questions as the Exemption Bill. On December 20, 1862, she wrote Curry that she was disappointed to see that his speeches (copies of which he had mailed to her) did not contain his views on the Exemption Bill, "which has caused such general dissatisfaction and which seems destined, I fear, to prove our politico-social *At*e." She continues, "In the unfortunate absence of that publicity of congressional debate, for which Mr. Yancey struggled so powerfully, the odium of an unpopular measure is unjustly and indiscriminately heaped on all who chance to constitute our Congress," including Curry himself. She describes the "spirit of insubordination and disaffection which is rife in our armies," but fortunately the newspapers have "judiciously" refrained from reporting "the disgraceful truth" of conditions. "The number of desertions in General Pemberton's army, and even among the troops stationed in Alabama, is appalling."[67]

The wrongs of the Exemption Bill cannot be corrected by the horrible punishments inflicted upon the deserters, she insists. Her sympathies lie entirely with the common soldiers, "who plead in palliation of desertion, the cries of hungry wives and starving children" who are unable to work the fields or to secure food and clothing. The real enemies of the Confederate war effort are the "shameless tribe of speculators and extortioners" who have brought about high prices. The Exemption Bill even protects such profiteers, she argues, for it "offers premiums for extortion among all classes of artificers, instead of compelling them either to join the ranks of the army, or furnish such necessities as shoes and meal at reasonable rates."

Another serious cause of disaffection among the troops, she points out, is the suspicion that Southern men are called from their work to serve in the army in order to protect the property of slave-holders, who often escape conscription under the Exemption Bill. She cites a case of open rebellion in St. Clair County, Alabama, against the abuses of the infamous bill: a band of three hundred furloughed soldiers had a meeting and swore to remain at home, even if it meant armed resistance against arresting officers. She tells Curry that the new session of Congress must correct the flaws in this badly timed legislation, which might never have been enacted if the people had heard it debated in open session.

Augusta Evans's services as a nurse during the early months of the war were reported to General P. G. T. Beauregard, hero of the Confederacy at the time, who had issued the order to fire on Fort Sumter and had later commanded key positions at the Confederate victories near Manassas. As a token of appreciation for her work, General Beauregard made her a present of his personal writing pen. On August 4, 1862, she acknowledged the tribute:

General Beauregard:
With heart throbbing with pleasure, and surely pardonable pride, I avail myself of the very earliest opportunity to attempt an expression of my earnest, cordial thanks for the exceedingly flattering testimonial of remembrance you so kindly conferred on me, through the courtesy of Colonel Roman. I can imagine no compliment more delicate and valuable than that which you have so unexpectedly paid me; your consecrated Sword is the Nation's, and your Pen, around whose diamond point cluster such hallowed associations, has now become the property of one, who although undeserving of so distinguished a mark of favor, is at least fully capable of the most intense and lasting appreciation of your kindness. Believe me, General Beauregard, I am inexpressibly gratified by this priceless token of a friendship I had not sufficient presumption to hope for, but will most earnestly endeavor to deserve.[68]

The letter continues for about two thousand additional words, in which the young authoress cites much abstruse erudition and quotes most generously. In response to the General's high praise for her writing, she complains of the minor role assigned to women in the building of the Confederacy: ". . . I have consoled myself with the reflection that, after all, woman's sphere of influence might be like Pascal's 'one of which the centre is everywhere, the circumference nowhere'; and though debarred from the 'tented field,' the cause of our beloved, struggling Confederacy may yet be advanced through the agency of its daughters." She encloses a copy of an article by herself (as yet unidentified) and makes reference to another, entitled "Memoria in Asternia," which she had mailed to the

General a fortnight before. These are but two of numerous unsigned articles which Augusta published in Southern newspapers on subjects relating to literature and the war.

In her witty apology for the length of this letter, Augusta says that Beauregard will probably have the same feeling toward her letter that "Sheridan's servant" had on the occasion of his master's "celebrated three-days-speech in the Warren Hastings trial," when the servant observed that the most eloquent passage of the address was the closing passage, "I have done, my Lords, I have done."

One of Miss Evans's shorter pieces of wartime journalism has been found in the correspondence of J. L. M. Curry, whose papers are now carefully indexed in the Library of Congress. The article, bearing the classical title of "The Mutilation of the Hermae," appeared on November 9, 1862, in the *Gulf City Home Journal,* a Mobile paper.[69] The major portion of this erudite propaganda is an account of "one of the most remarkable riddles which the Sphinx of history propounds," the mutilation of the marble images of Hermes which stood before many of the dwellings in ancient Athens, a sacrilege which took place in 415 B. C., on the eve of the Athenian expedition against Sicily. With an impressive array of scholarly terms, the author presents the setting and offers an explanation for the incident. Her propaganda is reserved for the final paragraphs, in which she uses bombastic rhetoric in a comparison of this ancient sacrilege with "the mutilation of the American Constitution by the depraved and unprincipled politicians of the North . . . The civilized world gazes in amazement at their unblushing and fanatical sacrilege." The destruction of "Black Republicanism" can be achieved only through the success of "Southern Confederacy."

During the course of the war Miss Evans and her mother made several dramatic journeys to the battlefields. On June 26, 1861, Augusta wrote her close friend, Rachel Lyons, from Norfolk, where she and her mother had arrived in search of the Third Alabama Regiment, to which Howard and Vivian Evans were attached.[70] She hoped to see her brothers before the yankee attack occurred, which was expected "very soon." The two women remained in this dangerous area nearly two months. Augusta seemed to relish the excitement of an imminent battle, if we may judge from the tone of her remarks. She relates a trip to Sewell's Point, where she went to visit "some Georgia friends" encamped there:

> . . . During my stay [we] went to an exposed point to take a look at Fortress Munroe, immediately opposite to us. While I stood looking at its savage portholes the immense Rifle Cannon at the Rip-Raps thundered angrily, and to our amazement, a heavy shell exploded a few yards from us. I turned my glass at once on the Rip-Raps, and distinctly saw the muzzle of the villainous gun pointed at our party; saw the gunmen at work reloading, and while I watched a second flash sent its missile of death right at us. When a third ball whizzed over our heads and exploded in a field just beyond us, the officers insisted we should get out of sight, as they were very evidently firing at us, and our lives were in danger. Oh! I longed for a secession flag to shake defiantly in their teeth at every fire; and my fingers fairly itched to touch off a red hot ball in answer to their chivalric civilities. Ten shells fell on land, but nobody was hurt, thank God.

Several days later, Augusta and a party of Confederates actually made a trip to the Northern stronghold at Fortress Munroe! She relates that a number of persons in Norfolk, "afflicted with Northern birth and Northern proclivities," were eager to return to "old Abe's mantle," and General Huger prepared to send them to Fortress Munroe in a tugboat under a flag of truce. Augusta and several friends were invited to make the exciting trip. She wrote Rachel Lyons:

> I went down with two or three friends and had a fine view of the Fortress, Rip-Raps, Hampton, Newport News, and all other points of interest. We lay for three hours right under the 60 guns of the flagship "Minnesota" and were very near the traitorous "Cumberland," "Monticello," "Anacostia," and others. The day was one of the most eventful of my life and I think I shall never forget it. While we waited for Butler to receive his precious cargo of renegades, the Rip-Raps opened fire on our battery at Sewell's Point. We stopped on our return to the city and sent a boat ashore to know whether any injury was effected, but "nobody hurt" was shouted back, amid bursts of laughter from the gunners.

The closeness of battle to the daily lives of Southerners is revealed in another letter to Rachel, dated May 31, 1862, in which Augusta states that her father and mother "have been absent from home for two weeks, waiting in the vicinity of Corinth [Mississippi], so as to be near my Bother [Howard] in case he were wounded . . ."

Two years later Augusta accompanied her aunt, Mrs. T. C. Evans, to Virginia once more, this time to investigate the reported death of her cousin, William S. Evans, in the Battle of Chancellorsville. Fortunately, the women found the boy alive.

In the early autumn of the same year, 1863, Augusta and her mother again sought Howard Evans just before an impending battle. One sentimental incident in this journey has been told many times by friends and relatives of the novelist, and perhaps its flavor is best preserved in the language of another unreconstructed rebel, Mrs. LaSalle Pickett:

> With the beautiful voice which so enchanted me, she once took captive General Bragg's army on Lookout Mountain. With her mother she had gone to visit her brother, Captain Howard Evans, just before the battle of Chickamauga. It chanced that he had been sent to the front before they arrived, but they were hospitably received and given a hut on the slope. At midnight they were awakened by steps and whispers and upon inquiry found that their unexpected visitors were soldiers who had crept through the lines to see Miss Evans and hear her sing. The mother was disposed to object to her appearing at a time and place not conventionally appropriate to artistic performances, but, wrapping her travelling coat and robe about her, she went out into the moonlight with her mass of hair streaming in the wind like a flying cloud, and sang that thrilling song written by her friend, Randall, "Maryland My Maryland." . . . When the song was finished the sobs and cheers that burst from the soldier-hearts formed an encore not to be denied, and again that battle-cry thrilled out upon the air. The moment of silence that followed was broken by the high, shrill, quavering, penetrating note of the rebel yell.[71]

Augusta had a personal interest in the song and its author, James Ryder Randall. "Maryland, my Maryland" became the marching song of the Confederacy, a lyric characterized by Oliver Wendell Holmes as "the greatest war song of any nation . . . My only regret is that I could not do for Massachusetts what Randall did for Maryland."[72] At the time of his composition of the lyric (the music is from an old German folk song, best known as the tune of "Tannenbaum, O Tannenbaum"), Randall was a frequent visitor at Augusta Evans's house in Mobile, where he came to court her younger sister, Caroline Cooper Evans, then nineteen years of age. He was residing at Pointe Coupee, Louisiana, where he taught English literature at Poydras College and contributed occasionally to the local newspaper. In April, 1861, Randall's chief interests, though, were the writing of poems and the courtship of Caroline. The couple became engaged, but their families persuaded them to postpone the marriage indefinitely because of the poor health of both the girl and the poet. After the war Caroline married Colonel Bush Jones, and Randall married Katherine Hammond.

In May, 1862, Augusta wrote Rachel about a visit of Randall and their mutual friend, Henry Timrod, to Georgia Cottage. She calls Randall "our noblest young Southern Poet, whose magnificent appeals to poor Maryland have so stirred the heart of our people." She is impressed by Henry Timrod, whose nature is as "skrinking and sensitive as a mimosa, but his native reticence wears away as I know him better." Randall, however, made a more forceful impression: "[He is] the very antipodes of your quiet friend. Randall is a rich, rare, tropical, luxuriant soul, whose beautiful thoughts and glowing images overflow continually, like a silver winecup whose amber and purple foam oozes over the brim. A refugee from his home in New Orleans, he is of course rather sad just now, but I trust better, brighter days are in store for us all."

One of Randall's sentimental love poems, "The Damsel of Mobile," was probably written to Caroline Evans. The last stanza is somewhat more graceful than the others:

> I know, I know that Summer goes,
> Like some divine disguise;
> I know that Summer rapture flows
> By ringlets and blue eyes—
> But thou, My Psyche and my soul!
> To thee alone I kneel,
> With the Summer sunshine in thy hair,
> Darling Damsel of Mobile![73]

War work absorbed much of Augusta's time and energy, but her letters to Rachel Lyons reveal the lighter side of her nature, a more girlish and natural feature of her character than ever emerges from her books. Here we find her wholesome delight in the attentions of dashing officers whom she met at Camp Beulah or in the company of her brothers. In February, 1864, she wrote Rachel about a strenuous and exciting train ride across Alabama, which she made with Ellen Muldon and Frank Crawford—the latter a girl, who later shocked many Mobilians by divorcing her first husband and marrying the fabulous capitalist, "Commodore" Cornelius Vanderbilt, though this breach of Victorian morality apparently did not injure Augusta's friendship with her. Confederate provost marshalls frequently stopped the three girls, but Augusta's credentials kept them moving; finally, they reached Pollard, Alabama, where a stern officer delayed them. The rigors of war-time regulations did not depress them, if we may judge by the letter written by Augusta, who described the whole trip as a happy lark. "A gentleman stepped up, took *that basket* and Ma's shawl and asked permission to show us to the only place of refuge." At a fireside in the railway station they found "*fifteen gentlemen* and two other forlorn ladies. Here we sat up till sunrise, when Captain Minge came down and carried us up to his house where we remained during the rest of our impromptu visit to Pollard. I have spent many pleasant hours, but I think I never enjoyed anything more keenly than I did the conversation that took place during our sitting up. Many of the gentlemen were officers, all were intelligent, some remarkably witty. I never heard as many brilliant things said in the same length of time, and I am sure, I never laughed as much before . . . I knew none of the party but they all seemed to know me."[74]

The next morning General Maury telegraphed from Mobile: "Allow Miss Evans to come at once to Mobile." This dispatch gave sufficient priority for the passage of all three girls.

If Augusta suffered deeply over her broken engagement to James Reed Spaulding, her letters do not reveal it. However, she probably would have refrained from admitting disappointment in writing to such an attractive belle as Rachel Lyons, whose hand was sought by numerous suitors. Augusta liked to boast of her popularity with the officers: "If you only knew how constantly I am interrupted by company . . . Morning, noon, and night my ears are greeted with the sound of 'Miss Gusta, somebody is coming up the walk.' Last night there were *six gentlemen* here till 12 o'clock."[75]

She admits that Sallie (her sister, Sarah, then twenty years of age) helped to entertain this group, but she makes it clear that other officers paid special attention to her. She hopes that the departing Confederates will return soon, especially Mr. Lovelace—"I shall miss Mr. Lovelace very much indeed," she confesses to Rachel. Then she speaks of her friendship with a Captain Cox and their mutual friend, "Healy, the Louisiana artist." At other times she entertained "General Quarles," "Major Commings," "Captain Holland," "Major Thomas," and "Captain Godfrey." One day "Tennessee Johnston, or rather Polk Johnston," came to Georgia Cottage and assisted Augusta and Captain Cox in tying up the vines to the tall trellises—"and saying brilliant things! which alas! for want of a Boswell! will not be preserved for the kind and tender public."[76] Was she assuming that this letter would reach the public eyes? Apparently.

Some of these young officers came to see the other Evans girls, no doubt, for Caroline and Sarah had their beaux, but on several occasions the prominent visitors called at Georgia Cottage to enlist Augusta's support in political or military matters. In her letter of January 27, 1864, to Curry, she describes a visit of Admiral Franklin Buchanan, who complained bitterly of the government's indifference to his requests for men to serve on the newly commissioned gunboat, the *Tennessee*. He needed 665 men and had placed many requisitions for them, but only twenty men had been sent by the Richmond authorities. It is clear that he expects Augusta Evans to do something about it, and she argues the Admiral's cause eloquently in her letter to Curry, as if she expected the politician to take some action. In the following months the *Tennessee* received a reasonable proportion of its complement of men, for the gallant iron-clad ram fought stubbornly against Farragut's superior forces in the battle of Mobile Bay. Admiral Buchanan received a serious wound in the action, and Augusta's friend who helped her tie up the vines, "Tennessee Johnston," commanded the clumsy vessel with great skill and daring.

CHAPTER IX

Macaria

1863-1864

"To the Brave Soldiers of the Southern Army"

FROM JUNE of 1862 to March of the following year, Augusta devoted every spare moment to the writing of a novel which she hoped would bring glory to the Confederacy and would lift the morale of the Southland. Many portions of the book were written on scraps of wrapping paper as she sat beside the hospital cots of Camp Beulah. She not only wished to present a favorable picture of life in the South before and during the war, but she hoped to do for her own cause what Thomas Paine had done for the Patriot position in the Revolution—to emphasize the new nation's victories, to minimize its setbacks, to evaluate the strength of the Confederate government, and to warn the leaders against certain dangers. Many passages of *Macaria* serve as touchstones of patriotism, as reminders that the times will certainly "try men's souls." All references to this novel and to Augusta's labors in writing it are couched in reverent tones, as if she and her critics considered the composition as a kind of mission.

Early in 1863 she informed General Beauregard of her project and requested him to give her an outline of the great Confederate victories at Manassas. Perhaps the most flattering tribute to Miss Evans's wartime services is the confidence which this general placed in her abilities as a propagandist. In the midst of a crucial year in the war, Beauregard interrupted his military labors and composed an account of the early battles in Virginia, which he knew would be ably utilized in the forthcoming *Macaria.*

On March 24 the General wrote Miss Evans that his "reports of the Battles of Bull Run and Manassas" were being forwarded, "not copied however to my satisfaction, but for fear of further delays I send them as they are by the Southern Express Company."[77] The original manuscript of these "reports" has not been found, but Augusta's account of the battles in Chapter XXX probably follows Beauregard's outline closely.

When *Macaria* was completed, Augusta sent the manuscript to the firm of West and Johnson in Richmond, Virginia, who had the book printed on crude wrapping paper; the boards used in the binding were covered with wall paper, the only materials available at the time. The printing was done by Walker, Evans, and Cogswell of Columbia, South Carolina. This Confederate edition is dated 1863 and is now a rare collector's item.[78] Shortly after its appearance, the author smuggled a copy to her New York publisher by a blockade runner via Cuba, and he made arrangements with J. B. Lippincott to issue a Northern edition in a binding uniform with that of the earlier success, *Beulah.* Derby relates in his memoirs that another publisher, "one Michael Doolady," had already begun printing an edition of *Macaria*.[79] Still a loyal friend of Miss Evans in spite of her politics, Derby called on Doolady and asked what royalty he had arranged to pay the author, and the reply was given that "the author being an arch rebel was not entitled to copyright and would receive none." Derby sent for Lippincott, who came up from Philadelphia to add his protest against such piracy, and the outcome was that Doolady was given the choice of paying royalties to the author, which would be held in trust by Derby until the end of the war, or of competing with a rival edition to be issued immediately by Lippincott. He chose to pay the royalties, of which we shall hear later.

Both editions of *Macaria* found ardent admirers and vigorous detractors. One historian states that the work was "the most popular novel published in the South during the war."[80] Its value as propaganda was recognized immediately by the enemy, for General G. H. Thomas, who commanded a Federal army in Tennessee, pronounced it "contraband and dangerous," banned it among the Yankee troops, and burned all copies which he found.[81]

The first half of *Macaria* covers the years immediately preceding Secession. A reader who is unaware of the propagandistic motive of the author may find few materials in the early pages which distinguish this book from other novels of domestic sentimentalism—the same moralizing, the familiar pathetic situations, a narrative with greater emphasis upon rewards for virtue and punishments for misconduct than upon realistic handling of character and action. The protagonists are virtuous, dignified people whose homelife, social standards, treatment of slaves, and interest in public affairs are models of propriety and cultural refinement —in short, they are idealized Southerners who are made to conform to a propagandist's morale-building picture of the South before and during the war. In the first twenty-six chapters, the author's aloofness from political questions enhances the effect of her propaganda, for the Southern reader would be impressed with the necessity of protecting such gentility and peace as the author describes, and the Northern reader would begin to question the accuracy of charges made by Mrs. Stowe, Seward, Garrison, Hinton Helper, Theodore Parker and others.

The war chapters in *Macaria,* covering the last one hundred and twenty pages, fulfill the promise of the dedication: "To the Brave Soldiers of the Southern Army." This section presents a zealous defence of Southern leadership and a full statement of the ideals for which Confederates believed they were fighting. Other passages, less rational perhaps but more memorable as propaganda, are enriched with the author's command of sentimental effects: scenes dramatizing the departure of friends, sons and brothers; accounts of housewives sewing diligently or directing the manufacture of goods for troops;[82] touching recitals of the work of loyal slaves who remain near their mistresses and till the soil; narratives of other courageous slaves who accompany their masters into battle; and stirring tributes to the generals and to the "private in the ranks." Hackneyed though it is, the description of a bullet's striking the heroine's ambrotype, which is carried in the breast-pocket of the hero, thus saving his life, is good war-time propaganda. This passage may be the basis for the well circulated story that the life of a Confederate was saved when another yankee bullet was stopped by a copy of *Macaria,* also carried over the rebel's heart.[83]

These emotional materials from the daily lives of a people at war are buttressed by authentic accounts of Confederate victories and heroic episodes. One highly romantic incident is undoubtedly taken from Beauregard's letter and notes: Miss Evans relates with much emotion the flight of "a young lady of Washington" through the Federal lines, carrying secret information "in the twist of her luxuriant hair" which would inform Beauregard and Johnston "of the designs of McDowell and the archapostate, Scott."[84] In his letter to Miss Evans, General Beauregard describes an identical service rendered by a "Miss Duval of Washington," who brought information through the lines on July 10, 1861, which enabled Beauregard to prepare his forces to meet "the positive advance of the enemy across the Potomac." His letter contains details which were apparently omitted in the "reports":

I then immediately commenced making my preparations to receive his mediated attack and I sent one of my aids (Col. J. S. Preston) to communicate the information received to the Pres. [Jefferson Davis] as well as my future operations. On the night of the 16th of July, I received by special messenger (a Mr. Donnellan) the second dispatch (in cypher of Mrs. G.) telling me that the enemy—55,000 strong, I believe—would positively commence that day his advance from Arlington Heights and Alexandria on to Manassas, via Fairfax courthouse and Centreville. Early the next morning

I telegraphed this information to President Davis. About noon I received his telegram to order Gen. Johnston to join his forces with mine. By that time, however, the enemy had already driven in by pickets in advance of Fairfax Courthouse and I answered the President that I feared it was then too late, but still would telegraph and send a messenger to Gen. Johnston. The latter arrived about noon on the 20th. At about 4:30 A.M. sent my final orders to commence the movement (see my report of the battle of Manassas), Gens. Ewell and Holmes on the right, to start first to attack and turn the enemy's left and rear at Centreville. At about 8:30 A.M. having given all preliminary orders I left my headquarters with Gen. Johnston for the scene of action near Mitchel's Ford at Bull Run. At about 10:30 I was informed by a messenger from Gen. Ewell (a gallant and meritorious officer) that he had not yet received directly my orders to advance but would do so at once from information received to that effect from Gen. D. R. Jones, next on his left, and who was to have followed his movements.[85]

It was too late, Beauregard adds, because the enemy was already gaining ground on his left. The whole plan of battle was changed on the spur of the moment, and green troops had to be ordered to the first line of defence. "My heart for a moment failed me," the general confesses. "I felt as though all was lost, and I wished I had fallen in the battle of the 18th. But I soon rallied and I then solemnly pledged my life that I would that day conquer or die." These are the words of a man who believes that his correspondent can give future generations an accurate account of his great moment in history. He adds that his raw troops fought valiantly—"the enemy commenced flying about 4:30 P.M., and the President arrived on the field about half an hour later, in time however to enjoy that agreeable sight."

The treatment of political issues in *Macaria* is as

biased as the prejudices underlying the emotional scenes —that is, it suits the requirements of wartime propaganda. Here and there the author and her leading characters refer to the North as a land of "shameless, hideous Abolitionism," harassed by a mob of zealots who would put the South in "Yankee Egyptic bondage." Lincoln's minions have begun the "iniquitous task of . . . setting aside all constitutional forms"; the press of the North is "muzzled," and "habeas corpus is no more." Liberty has "fled from her polluted fane" and seeks protection "on the banner of the Confederacy." The name "Union" has become "everywhere a symbol of political duplicity." The enraged people of the North, "hireling hordes of oppression," are blinded by "avarice and hate," and would exercise over the South the same intolerance and bigotry that characterized Puritanism in "the Cain-cursed race of New England."[86]

On the other hand, the South—"the bodyguard for the liberty of the Republic"—is calm and confident. All blame for Secession rests upon the government at Washington, for Southern leaders tried "honorably" to withstand Northern "political despotism," but were forced to withdraw when their Constitutional rights were ignored by the party of Lincoln. Since all "just governments rest upon the consent of the governed," the South had no choice but to accept the "Revolution" and fight for her "Independence." Because of the "stern resolution and self-abnegation" of Southern women and the "God fearing prayer" and bravery of Southern men, success is assured.[87]

This direct propaganda is enforced with arguments

which would appeal especially to the thoughtful conservatives in the South. The hero of *Macaria,* Russell Aubrey, warns Southern leaders that the "hydra-headed foe of democracy, . . . demagogism," is responsible for Northern Abolition sentiment. To throttle the power of the demagogues and preserve the Southern way of life, he proposes that suffrage among foreign born be limited, that a property clause be a requisite for voting, that the judiciary be appointed for life, and that the President's term of office be lengthened. The neglect of such restrictions upon expanding "demagogism" was the cause of Lincoln's election, the author appears to argue through her hero, and Secession was the result of not listening to the advice of Southern conservatism.[88]

That such reactionary political views are those of the author, and not merely of a representative Confederate hero, is evident from Miss Evans's letters to Curry in 1863 and 1864. She frequently attacks the evils of "demagogism," and when Curry was defeated in 1863 for his seat in the Confederate Congress, she blamed an unappreciative and uninformed electorate.[89] "Universal suffrage," she argues, "is an effete theory of Utopian origin, which might find acceptation in the shadowy realms of *Bensalem* but certainly not in this sternly-real, rushing, *explosive* 19th Century."

Her pessimism with regard to popular democracy in the Confederacy could not be expressed openly in *Macaria,* if this book was to boost the morale of the new republic, but she does not hesitate to tell Curry her views on the unenlightened public. In January, 1864, she sees the danger of the South's forgetting the principles for which she went to war, "and many are now willing to glide unhesitatingly into a dictatorship, a military despotism—even into a state of colonial dependence, with gradual emancipation [of slaves] a condition of foreign [i.e. Northern] intervention and protection." The "palpable blunders of the Administration" are evident to all, but the "people are rocking from their former firm faith in democratic republicanism." The recent elections in Alabama show the low ebb of public opinion, she argues, for the results indicate that "the polls are controlled by sordid, intriguing shallow-brained 'Cooperation' reconstructionists."[90]

The last chapters of *Macaria* present a detailed discussion of the dangers which beset the Confederacy. "Demagogism" and "nepotism" must be obliterated before the new nation can fulfill her destiny. The possibility of Secession among the Confederate states can be avoided by courageous leadership and wise legislation. (The question of the right to secede is omitted in the Confederate Constitution.) A few specific proposals are made: (1) "chemical" preservation of the soil will forestall agricultural unrest and discourage migrations to new lands in the West; (2) the hateful "protection" system of tariffs will be avoided by discouraging the establishment of factories in the South; (3) Southern ports will be opened to free trade—except to the markets of "Lincolndom"; (4) Congress will be given the power to appoint cabinet members and diplomats; and (5) Confederate presidents will be elected for their "intrinsic ability and nobility of soul," not because they are submissive "party-machine" candidates. These "reforms," together with the absence of "antagonistic systems of labor," will curtail the power of demagogues and will insure Confederate solidarity.[91]

A platform of this kind, proposed by one who was in close touch with the makers of policy, throws much light upon the inconsistencies in Confederate economics, particularly the weird mixture of progressive and reactionary thinking with respect to cotton, fertilizer, manufacturing, and free trade.

Macaria received the attention of both Southern and Northern reviewers in 1864, but the limited wartime editions prevented the novel from reaching the widespread audience which had acclaimed *Beulah*. It was composed as the author's dutiful memorial to a cause she loved, though its rhetoric probably has less appeal today than do other sentimental qualities which readers have always sought in the works of Augusta Evans. The Confederate propaganda of *Macaria* is certainly not out of place in a sentimental view of the past, but the practical values of its persuasive passages have merged, probably disappeared, in the novel's contribution to the romantic myth in which the North and the South have embalmed the War Between the States.

CHAPTER X

Crusader for a Lost Cause

1864-1867

IN HER SPIRITED contributions to the Confederacy, Miss Evans reached a status among the leaders of her region which was uncommon for a woman at that time. She was accepted not only as a valued moulder of public opinion but as an equal among the new nation's influential statesmen. The best evidence of such high esteem is found in her correspondence with J. L. M. Curry, Confederate congressman and later preacher and educator.

In 1862 she wrote him concerning her opinions on the removal of General Forney and the appointment of General Buckner as commanding officer at Mobile. In the same letter she discussed the defences of Mobile, the dangers of the Exemption Bill, the advantages of open debate in the Confederate Congress, and the prevalence of desertion in the army.[92] Not many women of the era were in a position to offer sound advice on such a variety of subjects.

Perhaps the best indication of her influence over Curry is seen in his request that she criticize the subject of a speech which he intended to deliver in Richmond during the summer of 1863: "Is the character of Southern women prejudicially affected by slavery?" Arguments of this type always stimulated Augusta, and she replied with a full analysis of the subtle question, honestly admitting that history offers little or no proof that free women have benefited from the leisure which slavery has made possible. Just "entre nous," she writes, "it appears that the physical and mental status of Southern women" are adversely affected by the institution. Are not the women in the households of slave-owners, as a class, "enervated, lethargic, incapable of enduring fatigue . . . afflicted with chronic lassitude? Why? Simply because they never systematically exercise." The average Southern housewife who enjoys the advantages of slave ownership is a useless "incubus to her husband and utterly incapable of properly educating and attending to her children." The leisure which she has is not properly used, and her freedom from work has contributed to her bad health. Southern women are often pleasant and graceful, she admits, but their "information is painfully scanty, their judgment defective, their reasoning faculties dwarfed, their aspirations weak and frivolous." The history of nations in other southern climes where slavery has flourished gives the same account of its women.[93]

But this is not a timely or a remunerative subject, Augusta tells the statesman. Why not address the people in the Confederate capital on the topic: "Political and Social Quicksands of the Future"? She reminds Curry that there are "mouldering mournful ruins which darken the past of Republics." Even now she sees in her land the effects of corruption, "grim and merciless as Carlyle's 'Utilitaria.'" To plead for the reform of evils "seems the *imperative* duty of our statesmen." The Constitution must be changed, and the people must be educated to accept "restrictions of our suffrage," or the South will be "plunged into hopeless anarchy."

To a reader in our age, such conservatism appears to be out of character when uttered by a person who had experienced poverty and had known few of the advantages of the planter class, but the views of Southern Bourbonism were closely allied to the "tradition" or the "cause" which the South was defending. Fear of political power in the hands of the masses was common among those who looked with suspicion upon the growth of industrialism, which was dependent upon masses of laborers who were usually unenlightened. At the time that she was expressing her fears to Curry, Augusta was composing her war novel, *Macaria,* in which she reveals the great dangers of "demagogism." She undoubtedly knew that Curry, a spokesman for the planter class, would know how to attack those leaders who favored universal suffrage of white men and who respected the prejudices of the masses.

Modestly, the young woman offers the statesman a little book which she believes will help to shape his thoughts in the direction that she suggests. She identifies it as "'Reflections on the Rise and Fall of Ancient Republics' by Montagne." She states that she had considered republishing it, with her own "analytical sketch of our old Republic," but she wonders if she has the competence for such a task.

Curry listened to her advice, discarded the untimely

subject of the effect of slavery on Southern womanhood, and lectured on the "social quicksands of the future." Several months later, Augusta wrote him that she was pleased to hear that the Richmond audience received his message with enthusiasm.[94]

Early in their correspondence Miss Evans had apparently urged Curry to seek the passage of an equitable copyright act in the Confederate Congress. In her letter of July 15, 1863, she thanks him for his "friendly interest and perseverance" in the enactment of the "act securing copyrights," and she assures him that the new law will be satisfactory to Southern authors.

Many women in public life today—enjoying better communications and more sympathetic public relations than Augusta Evans experienced—would be envious of the breadth of this young woman's interests. In her letters to Curry she freely analyzed the faulty reasoning of John Stuart Mill's *Political Economy,* and she attacked vigorously the "effete theory" of universal suffrage. Then she turned to the battles of the current war and drew a unique comparison between the campaigns of McClellan and those of the German strategist, Wallenstein; likewise, she noted parallels between Stonewall Jackson's tactics and those of Gustavius Adolphus. At the beginning of Reconstruction, she was brave enough to record her fears on the dangers of "military despotism."

Another instance of the confidence which men in high estate placed in Miss Evans is the record of a letter from Senator Benjamin H. Hill of Georgia, in which he confides to her his fear of disunion in the Confederacy in February, 1865. Somehow, this letter was allowed to be published in the Columbus (Ga.) *Sun,* on March 26, 1865. Hill's biographer states that Miss Evans acted "in rather bad faith, or at least carelessly"; but there is no proof that she is responsible for the publication of the letter. It is true that the incident must have been embarrassing to a man in Hill's position, particularly since it appeared only two weeks before the surrender at Appomatox.[95]

During the dark days of Reconstruction, Augusta did not seek forgetfulness of defeat through exaggerated loyalty to the past. Not that she did not feel the defeat very intensely, as evidenced in a letter to Curry: "I believe I loved our cause *as a Jesuit his order;* and its utter ruin has saddened and crushed me, as no other event of my life had power to do."[96] But rather, her days were so filled with practical chores and her nights with so much hope and planning that little time was left for inert sentimental reminiscences. The biographer of Robert Toombs, the first Confederate Secretary of State, describes a gentle service which Miss Evans rendered to Toombs when he was a fugitive rebel General, trying to escape from Northern troops. Augusta's father and brother were old friends of Toombs, and in the spring of 1865 he sought refuge in their house during his flight through Mobile. The Evans servants had fled, and though Augusta had little skill in the kitchen (as she often admitted in later years), she prepared Toombs's meals to the best of her ability. She assumed responsibility for his security and considered it a privilege to wait upon him.

While Toombs was still with the Evans family, a Northern officer stopped at their house and remarked to Augusta, in the presence of others, that he was sure he had seen General Toombs near Mobile a few days before. Augusta came to the rescue of her shocked parents with the quick retort that she "had heard" that Toombs was in Cuba!

The secret visit of this prominent Confederate is described as "the most agreeable episode in the hunted man's long exile." His biographer speaks of Toombs's fondness for the companionship of intellectual women, and Augusta's talents in conversation were remarkable. She was "a charming talker, as bright as a jewel, and Toombs was a Chesterfield with ladies. The General would walk to and fro along the shaded walks [at Georgia Cottage] and pour forth, in his matchless way, the secret history of the ruin of the Confederate hopes."[97]

Perhaps it was during these conversations that Miss Evans conceived the plan of writing a history of the Confederacy. On October 7, 1865, she wrote Curry a letter of thanks for his offer of "valuable Congressional documents." She confides to him, "My history I intend to make the great end of all my labors in the realm of letters." This project was soon abandoned in favor of the composition of *St. Elmo.*

Another practical project which Miss Evans managed at the close of the war was a campaign to raise funds for the removal of Mobilians from distant battlefields to Magnolia Cemetery in the Gulf city. Her committee succeeded in obtaining $1,500 at a time when the contributors often lacked the necessities of life.[98] In yankee greenbacks, this sum was the equivalent of many times its purchasing power today; it brought scores of fallen Confederates home.

Early in 1866 Miss Evans took an interest in another means of perpetuating the "Cause." She served as chairman for a drive to collect funds for the erection of a memorial monument to the Confederate dead. The campaign was conducted throughout the spring, and on June 22 she wrote Curry that a shaft of granite had been purchased, but she feared that the "Boards of Councilmen and Aldermen [were] too cowardly to risk giving umbrage to the 'powers that be' [the yankee army of occupation]." She wanted the monument placed in a prominent square, and she suggested that its inscription should be a simple one, like "to the Unknown Heroes who fell in the defence of our Homes." The completion of this memorial was not accomplished until 1874, when the shaft was erected in Magnolia Cemetery, bearing the simple inscription on all four sides, "The Confederate Dead."

On April 15, 1866, Augusta wrote Curry of another plan for honoring the Southern dead, which would have resulted in our first "Memorial Day" if she had sought organized support for her idea: "I intend to select some day in the year which will be reverently and tenderly consecrated to the melancholy task of ornamenting the graves and pronouncing eulogies upon the heroism and sublime endurance of their silent tenants."

The close of the war had brought poverty again to Augusta's family. Mr. Evans's health was declining rapidly, the older boys had been in the army for several years, and Augusta had received nothing from the Confederate publication of *Macaria.* The fall of Richmond had ruined the firm of West and Johnson, and the novelist understood that they could not "pay in greenbacks what they owed in Confederate money."[99] She confided in her friend Derby that her father had "lost everything; the slaves have been freed, and all our property confiscated." In her reference to "property," she must have meant Confederate bonds and the slaves; there is no record that other personal property or their real estate was seized.

Howard Evans, Augusta's favorite brother, came home in a serious condition from a wound he had received at the battle of Atlanta. His arm and shoulder were paralized, and an attack of typhoid fever left his memory impaired. Local doctors apparently offered little encouragement, so Augusta decided that Howard must be taken to New York so that "a German physician of celebrity" might examine him.[100] In the late summer of 1865 she and Howard secured passage in a steamer bound for New York.

Derby relates that Augusta called at his office shortly after her arrival, but she was so heavily veiled and her clothing was so worn and out-moded that he hardly recognized her. She told her publisher of the illness of her brother, who had modestly remained outside, "sitting on the steps"—probably suspicious of the reception the two ardent rebels would receive from the yankee businessman. Derby insisted that they stop at his house, and he begged Augusta to allow his wife to take care of Captain Evans during their stay. Her old friend also suggested, in his fatherly way, that she would probably want to shop for a new dress and bonnet before they drove out to his place. Augusta described the financial reverses they had suffered since the end of the war and confessed that she had no money with which to replenish her wardrobe. It was not until then that Derby realized that she was ignorant of the arrangements which he and Lippincott had forced upon Michael Doolady, the Northern publisher of *Macaria*. With much pride Derby announced the details of the agreement and admitted that a "considerable amount" of money was held by him from the Northern sales of this rebel novel. Augusta later said of Lippincott's generosity:

> I have always felt profoundly grateful to Mr. Lippincott, but fate has never indulged me in an opportunity of adequately thanking him for his generous and chivalric action, in behalf of an unknown rebel, who at that period was nursing Confederate soldiers in a hospital established near "Camp Beulah."[101]

On her return to Mobile from this short visit in the North, Augusta wrote Curry, "I was surprised at the kindness and courtesy shown me wherever I went." Every yankee she met was aware of her work for the Confederacy and of her unreconstructed views at this time, but all of them seemed willing to forgive her.[102] Her conduct on this trip, however, was not so gracious, as we shall see later.

The doctor whom they consulted in New York suggested treatment which gave Howard some relief from his paralysis, but his wound resulted in a permanently stiff shoulder. It was probably at this time that the very close companionship between Augusta and Howard began. She was only two years older than Howard, and they had shared very similar experiences and loyalties during the war. Twenty-six years later (in 1891), when Augusta's husband died and she decided to leave the beautiful estate where she and Colonel Wilson had been very happy, she persuaded Howard, who had remained a bachelor, to make his home with her during the remainder of their lives. Many older Mobilians still remember the frail couple who always took their walks together on Government Street, usually with arms filled with bonquets of flowers for the graves at Magnolia.

The sizeable bank account which Derby placed at Augusta's disposal was very useful in New York, but its value to the Evanses in Mobile was enormous. Credit was difficult to obtain in the war-weary city, and yankee greenbacks were scarce, particularly among Confederates like the Evanses who had lost heavily. Matt Evans's health was now so bad that he was virtually an invalid. Howard's injured arm was a handicap in seeking jobs, and Vivian Rutherford Evans, though twenty-six years of age, found that his status as veteran did not help much in obtaining work in a town that was dominated by the Federal army of occupation. Augusta's funds had to be stretched very far.

Unlike many of her sentimental compatriots, Augusta quickly realized that the Southern cause, as interpreted and defended by Confederates, was lost forever. She was always a consistent defender of ideals and loyalties, especially those traditionally identified with the South, but she was also a woman of much common sense. Leaders of the South must not overlook the perpetuation of principles for which many had died, she argued, and monuments must arise and books must be written. But Augusta saw that a new day had come, and though many believed that the South had been right all along, it was the duty of Southern leaders and authors to mould their messages in terms of post-bellum conditions.

Early in the year 1866 Augusta saw the wisdom of returning to the kind of writing which had made *Beulah* acceptable to thousands of Americans. She abandoned her plan to write a history of the Confederacy and began *St. Elmo,* the novel which made her famous. The single reference in this book to the recent war is made without bitterness. After such an active role in the conflict, why did she choose to ignore it in her most ambitious work? Perhaps she felt that her beloved constituency had suffered enough from the war, those of the South and the North. Or possibly she believed that she could lay greater emphasis upon the lasting values of former times, upon the noble impulses associated with good living in the ante-bellum South, if she developed the love story of Edna Earl and St. Elmo among stable, seemingly permanent conditions. In all of her books she is more concerned with *personal* joys and sorrows than with broader social conditions; even her attacks upon false standards in marriage, or upon the shallowness and misconduct in fashionable life, are presented through the effects of such evils upon noble people. Her view of reform agreed with

Emerson's thought: that reform should begin with the individual, not with "other people" or with society at large. So perhaps she believed that her message should not be forced to cope with the excitement of the national struggle.

An argument just as convincing as these, and much more practical, must have occurred to her also: novels of domestic sentimentalism always sell well. A book on the "secret history of the Confederacy" would have to be sensational in the extreme to compete in public sales with such lachrymose favorites as *The Wide, Wide World* or *The Lamplighter*. She had already demonstrated considerable talent for sentimental fiction, and she had every reason to believe that the public was eager to reward her in handsome royalties. If such were her thoughts when she undertook *St. Elmo,* few authors have been more prophetic.

The composition of her stout novel did not exhaust the energies of Augusta, then thirty years of age, for she found time to boost a promising literary journal published in New Orleans, the *Crescent Monthly*. She wrote Curry that she hoped to contribute articles on John Ruskin and Jean Ingelow, and she begged Curry to send the editor something from his own pen.[103] Her charitable efforts in behalf of the *Crescent Monthly* included a request to a "Colonel Taylor" that he write an essay on John Stuart Mill, and an appeal to Mr. Columbus Lee to submit an article on Buckle. The good will of these intellectuals was not sufficient nourishment for the ambitious journal, which offered its last issue in March, 1867, only twelve months after its founding.

Meanwhile, the manuscript of *St. Elmo* grew daily. Augusta's new publisher, G. W. Carleton, who had acquired Derby's control in the firm during the sixties, recognized the potential sale of the famous story and laid plans to set the type as rapidly as possible when the manuscript was completed. Early in December, 1866, advance copies of *St. Elmo* were placed in the hands of the reviewers.

CHAPTER XI

St. Elmo

1867

St. Elmo, the "most praised, best abused novel ever written," was received with mixed emotions, but everyone was amazed at the tremendous sales of the book. The appearance of several best sellers in the fifties had not conditioned the rapidly growing nation to the phenomenon of highly successful native literature. Bigness and popularity were hailed then, as now, as merits in themselves. And here was a bonanza worth talking about! Millions were reading it. One would think that the astonishing sales of *Uncle Tom's Cabin* (1852), or of Marion Harland's *Alone* (1854), or of Mary Jane Holmes's *Lena Rivers* (1856) would have prepared the times for the excitement of this new success. As if it were America's first best seller, the age felt a compulsion to perpetuate *St. Elmo* in various "material monuments," as one contemporary remarked, for it seemed that "only in a material way could the admirers of the book give adequate expression to their enthusiasm."[104]

There were steamboats and railway coaches named "St. Elmo." Many Southern towns had "St. Elmo Hotels," and at least two villages were named for the book. There was a "St. Elmo" punch, a very strong "St. Elmo" cigar, and several blue-ribboned dogs named "St. Elmo." Many country estates or city mansions were called "La Bocage," after the Murray estate in the novel. A remarkable number of children have been christened Edna Earl, for the heroine, or St. Elmo. And the latest honor for the novel is the naming of one of Mobile's finest camellias—"St. Elmo."

The popularity of the book was almost instantaneous. Two weeks after it reached the counters the publisher begged the eager public to be patient: "We are perfectly inundated with orders—and it is physically impossible to manufacture the books as rapidly as they are called for."[105] Shortly afterwards, the advertisements refer to *St. Elmo* "as a literary phenomenon," the demand for which could not be met with "five Adams presses running twenty-four hours each!"[106] Four months after publication a million people had read the novel, the publisher boasted.[107]

The absence of reliable records and indexes of sales before the year 1895 makes it impossible to establish the exact place of *St. Elmo* among all-time best selling novels, but it is safe to say that before the advent of book-of-the-month clubs, *St. Elmo* ran a close third to *Uncle Tom's Cabin* and *Ben-Hur*. In the year 1893 an effort was made to tabulate the reading tastes of the public, and *St. Elmo* was still a favorite, twenty-six years after its appearance. This novel was given a rating of 49 in a scale that ran as high as 92 for *David Copperfield*. It was judged to be more popular in that year than such works as *Oliver Twist, The Spy, Henry Es-*

mond, Tom Sawyer, and *Huckleberry Finn.*[108] The continued popularity of *St. Elmo* is attested by the number of editions available at bookstores as late as 1912, when nine publishers were offering thirteen issues, which ranged in price from 15c to $2.50. In 1928 the novel could be bought in six cheap issues, published by four firms. In the summer of 1949 *St. Elmo* made its appearance in one of the most popular cheap editions, bringing the number of editions in that year to four.

Before we leave the excitement of *St. Elmo's* reception, a word should be spoken in defence of the novel's reflection of the age in which it appeared. There is little realism in the book, and yet few novels have so much in common with the prejudices and emotions of their time. The paradox disappears when the broader aspects of the age are placed beside the prevailing impressions of this earnest melodrama.

The age was not ashamed of sentiment—it even gloried in it. The assumption that strong and earnest people obtain consolation through honest tears is implied in the folk songs, plays, religious services, domestic art, and politics of the period. Our ancestors in that era seldom doubted that *feeling* is an adequate gauge of good conduct and righteous beauty. A critic may apply learned terms to the doctrine—*sensibility,* for instance—and find sources in history and literature for its origin, but he will miss the power of its force unless he grasps the breadth and commonness of its influence, in evangelism, in frontier politics, in pioneer customs, and at the fireside of every American home. *St. Elmo* is as openly, as unashamedly sentimental as "Home Sweet

Home," or the dramatic version of "Rip Van Winkle," or the sermons at a camp meeting, or the democracy of Andy Jackson's followers. One look at the decorations on the walls of a characteristic Victorian parlor, or an hour spent with the yellowed pages of *Godey's Lady's Book* will reveal the frank pleasure which our ancestors obtained from reproductions of sentimental experience. The books and plays and sermons and pictures were cut from the same fabric of philosophy, but there were fewer sophisticates to smile when they were new, because the quality of sophistication differed at that time. Sentiment was fashionable.

St. Elmo was written for an age which expected oratory, not speeches, from its leaders; it was intended for an audience which took joy in applauding the elegant and impressive acting of Booth and McCullough—performances which ran the gamut of emotional expression. The book was addressed to people who were proud of dwelling in houses adorned with turrets, bay windows, and mazes of jig-saw atrocities which likewise approach the absurd—in the judgment of *today*. The book is a period piece; its opulence, though eccentric by any standard we can now imagine, reflects a hunger for culture that borders on the pathetic. We like to think that we are emancipated from all that today, but even the Victorians had a similar conceit of themselves, for they too believed that their standards were *modern*.

The hero of Miss Evans's romance has an ancestral home which is fitted out in the grand manner. There are Gothic windows of stained glass at La Bocage and a classical rotunda with "Moresque frescoes." A hot-house, with oriental pagoda roof, is surrounded by statues of Bacchus, Bacchante, and Triton. Grazing on the lawns are Himalayan and golden pheasant, bison, Lapland reindeer, scarlet flamingo, Cashmere goats, chamois, and a cow from Ava. The formal gardens are filled with Norway spruce and impenetrable hedges of osage orange. If all of these exotics appear a little out of place on a Southern plantation near Columbus, Georgia, we should not forget the oddities which customarily adorned many a Victorian great house; likewise, a similar taste for extravagance is revealed on every page of the annuals and gift-books which our grandparents bought for their parlor tables. It was a time when much was written about *sublimity* in art, architecture, and literature—particularly about the lofty sentiments of Oriental culture—but the minor artists and writers did not have the talent or imagination to follow the grand themes of the masters.

One late Victorian critic has shrewdly observed, "These novelists of the old type are handicapped for the future by the very excellences which made them popular in the past. Mrs. Wilson was a most vital expression of that Southern taste which, classical rather than imitative, flourished upon Meredith's *Lucile* and Bulwer's *The Lady of Lyons.*" He cites her "high seriousness of spirituality," her "picturesqueness of abstract statement," her deep love of scholarship, and her opulence of phrase, which help to make her "representative of a literary *genre* which, while it lasted, brought with it a healthy, wide enjoyment and an emotional appeal which, drawing plentifully upon warm sentiment treasured a romantic spirit the world would be poorer without."[109] Not only were the hero and heroine idealized in *St. Elmo,* but the setting was more elegant than life, and the style more refined than mere thinking.

St. Elmo was amazingly popular because it suited the tastes of the day, but one explanation of its vogue contains a puzzling contradiction. Charitable readers have always admitted that the novel has a tone of dedication, that the author's sincerity emerges from every page, but Miss Evans found it necessary to create a hero with sufficient evil in his early manhood to justify his salvation by a Christian heroine, and in so doing she innocently presents her reader with a rake so fascinating in his sinning that he "bowled over a whole generation of romantic schoolgirls," as one critic put it.[110] The object of Edna Earl's devout love is allowed to describe his sinfulness in her presence: "I drank, gambled, and my midnight carrousals would sicken your soul were I to paint all their hideousness. Whenever a brilliant and beautiful woman crossed my path I attached myself to her train of admirers, until I made her acknowledge my power and give public and unmistakable manifestations of her preference for me; then I left her—a target for the laughter of her circle."[111] All this because one woman, Agnes Powell, had secretly planned a loveless marriage with him for his money!

Many critics deplored Miss Evans's resurrection of such a familiar rake, but the triteness of the model had little effect upon public tastes. St. Elmo Murray may be a literary descendant of Guy Livingstone, or Tito in

Romola, or Rochester in *Jane Eyre,* or any one of Byron's cynical heroes, but his intriguing naughtiness was a sufficient attraction to overcome a distaste for his hackneyed qualities. One contemporary protested, "Once more we are bidden to listen to the story of the well-known gentleman who has exhausted every form of vice and excess, whose face is stamped with the lines of dissipation and care, who goes about the world breaking women's hearts . . . [A] charlatan of literature who is the central figure of Miss Evans's book—the gloomy being who lives in a mysterious chamber filled with Chaldee manuscripts, Turkish scimetars, and Eastern relics."[112] But then, as now, the public did not listen to such hyper-critical opinions.

At least one judicious critic indicated his preference for realism, rather than the gorgeous excesses so common at the time: "There is a certain degree of power exhibited in this volume [*St. Elmo*]," wrote a reviewer for the New York *Times,* "but it seems to us to be power misapplied. An American novelist might surely find a field for the exercise of the imagination apart from that which has been so long and so unprofitably occupied by the Corsair school of heroes. Is there nothing in the marvelous energy of our people to attract the attention of writers of fiction? Would it not be as easy to enlist our sympathies for the honest, sturdy lives led by the pioneers of civilization in the far West, as for the worn out type of *roués* which is the stock property of novelists of the present day."[113] In another decade Mark Twain understood what this critic wanted, and other notable realists followed, but Mrs. Wilson was never attracted to their standards of art.

The fact that nice Victorian girls and ladies were the chief admirers of St. Elmo's progress from sin to salvation will always be of interest to later generations whose critical standards are subtly, often innocently, swayed by Freudian principles. One cannot help wondering if such mildly rakish novels appealed to feminine tastes because Victorian women were so carefully sheltered from rational discussions of sex and sin. Recent literature has fully explored the frustrations and compulsions attributed to Victorian censorship in its many forms—and it probably did stimulate an appetite for narratives of lust and blasphemy—but the sensational aspects of the topic can easily lead us into errors of judgment not unlike those assigned to the modest feminine readers themselves. Arguments concerning thwarted emotional outlets of our forebears lose some of their attraction when we recall aspects of Victorianism as normally robustious as any moderate sensualist could wish: our ancestors' joy in Mark Twain's earthy humor, the generous laughter bestowed upon bawdy yarns at political rallies, meek acquiescence in the double standard of morality, and the popular acceptance of frontier buffooneries as recorded by A. B. Longstreet, Joseph Baldwin, Johnson J. Hooper, William T. Thompson, and many a newspaper wit who chose to be anonymous. The age respected the proprieties associated with virtuous, genteel conduct, but it often found release (we may even say *sublimation*) from the rigidities of Puritan standards through cock fights, horse races, tall tales, burlesques, prize fights, mistresses, vulgar pranks, and many more escapades which probably seemed more innocent in reality than they did in writing.

The man Augusta married, Colonel Lorenzo M. Wilson, had a keen relish for horse racing, but the strait-laced authoress certainly could not accept her tacit acquiescence in this hobby as a sign of compromise in her moral standards. Horse racing is a part of life, but literature should be above life. A novelist worthy of her prestige is not obliged to picture joy in horse racing, even though she permits her husband to receive genuine pleasure from it. More young men can be helped if authors place the racetrack in a category with intemperance and the minor sins. And Colonel Wilson probably saw nothing personal in his wife's distinctions. Literature was a moral trust to Augusta Evans Wilson, similar to the "call" of the ministry. As early as 1856 she wrote the Reverend Walter Harriss, "O! I want an artist, and glorious works of art that will fill my soul with God-born impulses! I want to soar not grovel with Calibans, Iagos! . . . A great and good man's life well told is a work of art; that is, of the art I love."[114] Her age honored her for the distinction and bought her books by the thousands.

Human curiosity about misconduct may have attracted many readers to the sardonic hero of *St. Elmo,* but there were thousands who read the book and then recommended it to others for the good that it would do them. Augusta's old friend, J. L. M. Curry, wrote her about the inspiration which he observed in the story, and she replied, "Indeed my dear Sir, I am inexpressibly gratified that you esteem *St. Elmo* so highly; and I trust that with the blessing of God, my 'labor will not be in vain,' and that I may be the humble instrument of doing some good, of leading some soul safely to Christ."[115]

Judging by the reminiscences of her friends, she was not disappointed in the novel's moral influence over her constituents. In the interviews which she granted after 1867, Mrs. Wilson stressed the hundreds of letters which came from all parts of this country and from foreign lands, thanking her "in sincere vein of personal gratitude for the practical good [her books] had done their writers in changing or shaping their lives." The following summary of this aspect of her popularity, written by a fellow Mobile novelist, Thomas Cooper DeLeon, expresses the sentiments of many American readers in the last century:

> I have read letters from all sections of our country . . . thanking Mrs. Wilson for her work . . . one and all bearing testimony to the high purity and simple Christianity of her men and women. And therein without delving deeper for hidden or needless reasons —is the real cause of the popularity today [in 1898] of these books, and of their first capture of the hearts of purer readers everywhere, despite the captiousness of critics and the flippancy of burlesquers. Mrs. Wilson writes to true men and women out of her heart of gold. She ever teaches the unanswerable lesson that right is right; that the touching of pitch defiles; that honesty is not only "the best policy," but the best duty as well.[116]

A more sophisticated critic of the period, Arthur B. Maurice of *Bookman*, ridicules the artistry of *St. Elmo,* but he concedes that the book is an excellent mirror of its time. In 1902 he wrote, "It has a significance much broader than its significance as a mere novel. In the literary development of many young Americans it has marked a stage, a period." [117] Eight years later he concludes, "Absurd as it too often is, there was not a line of it that was not inspired by a belief in lofty ideals and a passionate sincerity that checks the laughter on the lips . . . [*St. Elmo*] is not only not forgotten; it remains an early chapter in the code of life."[118]

Within eight months of its appearance, *St. Elmo* was honored with a parody, a thin little volume entitled *St. Twel'mo, or the Cuneiform Cyclopedist of Chattanooga*, written by the New York humorist, Charles Henry Webb. Augusta's friend, T. C. DeLeon, was convinced that Webb burlesqued the popular novel "in revenge for Miss Evans's flat refusal to meet him personally because he was on the New York *Times*, a Republican paper."[119] Such rudely consistent Southernism is apparently in disagreement with the sparse treatment of the war and attendant prejudices in *St. Elmo*, but DeLeon's account does jibe with a similar snub which occurred when Augusta took Howard Evans to New York in 1865. At a dinner given in her honor by Charles O'Connor, she refused to meet Henry J. Raymond, editor of the *Times*, because she could not forgive the violence of Raymond's editorials against the South.[120] One interesting factor in this little quarrel is that Raymond was the employer of James Reed Spaulding, whose proposal of marriage Augusta had rejected at the beginning of the war because of his Republican sympathies. In a letter to Curry, written immediately after her return to Mobile, she refers to the Raymond episode:

"Some of the prominent Republican leaders wished to see me, in order (so they say) 'to ascertain the true condition of affairs South,' but as I knew they were well acquainted with the entire success of their infamous subjugation programme, I positively refused to receive them."[121]

The parody, *St. Twel'mo,* achieves most of its humor through ridicule of Edna's innocent love for a rake and through ludicrous imitation of Miss Evans's erudition. In his introductory "Argument," Webb states, "If it be complained that . . . the reader cannot tell where the original ends and the travesty begins, certainly higher compliment, or more complete justification of puropse, could not fall to my lot."[122]

DeLeon states that Webb's parody gave much amusement to Augusta; however, such a friendly reception to adverse criticism was unusual with her. Perhaps her earnestness in writing fostered the assumption that her moralizing novels were above censure. During the next forty years she hurled many angry countercharges against her carping critics.

Most of the adverse criticism of *St. Elmo* is directed toward the author's pretentious elegance or "high seriousness" in the use of far-fetched allusions. Many of her passages offer perfect targets for the parodists, and Webb was not the only wit who made sport of such speeches as the following, in which St. Elmo tells Edna of his restless gloom:

I speak advisedly, for the true Io gad-fly, *ennue,* has stung me from hemisphere to hemisphere, across tempestuous oceans, scorching deserts, and icy mountain ranges. I have faced alike the bourrans of the steppes and the Samieli of Shamo, and the result of my vandal life is best epitomized in those grand but grim words of Bossuet: "*On trouve au fond de tout le vide et le neant.*" Nineteen years ago, to satisfy my hunger, I set out to hunt the daintiest food this world could furnish, and, like other fools, have learned finally, that life is but a huge mellow golden Osher, that mockingly sifts its bitter dust upon our eager lips. Ah! truly, *on trouve au fond le tout le vide et le neant!*[123]

In another passage the author brings up the interesting question of a girl's progress into adult maturity. It would seem that this common experience would demand simple language and homely comparisons, particularly in a novel of domestic sentimentalism, but Miss Evans chooses to describe Edna as standing "on the line, narrow and thin as Al-Sirat, that divides girlhood and womanhood," when "all seemed to her fresh, pure heart as inviting and bewitching as the magnificent panorama upon which enraptured lotopagi gazed from the ancient acropolis of Cyrene."[124]

This style was her conception of the grand manner; she was striving to create examples of the "purple patches" of eloquence so highly prized in the great prose of the day.

Occasionally a passage approaches eloquence in simpler ways, particularly when the author appears to be writing from intense conviction. Take the case of Augusta's views on woman's suffrage. Her opposition to this aspect of the feminist movement was based upon emotional considerations, not political theory. She was convinced that the exercise of too many "rights" would injure a woman's services in the home, would harden her character and render her less capable of performing the various tender offices which she felt were woman's principal duties in life. She shows the intensity of her feelings in this noble outburst which is placed in the mouth of her heroine:

I think, sir, that the noble and true women of this continent earnestly believe that the day which invests them with the elective franchise would be the blackest in the annals of humanity, would ring the death-knell of modern civilization, of national prosperity, social morality, and domestic happiness! and would consign the race to a night of degradation and horror infinitely more appalling than a return to primeval barbarism . . . God, the Maker, tenderly anchored womanhood in the peaceful, blessed haven of home; and if man is ever insane enough to mar the divine economy, by setting women afloat on the turbulent, roaring sea of politics, they will speedily become pitiable wrecks . . . Surely utter ignorance is infinitely preferable to erudite unwomanliness.[125]

Such conservatism undoubtedly contributed to the popularity of *St. Elmo.* It is interesting to note that other successful sentimental authors were in accord with Miss Evans on the question of votes for women. The New York *Times* reported in December, 1888, that Ella Wheeler Wilcox, Celia Thaxter, Mrs. E. D. E. N. Southworth, Louisa Chandler Moulton, Rose Terry Cooke, and Augusta Evans Wilson were quoted in a symposium as opposing woman's suffrage.[126] Their objections were similar to the views expressed by Edna Earl.

There are sound reasons for the contemporary attacks upon *St. Elmo* as a work of questionable artistic structure. It would be difficult for any novelist to achieve fictional unity from such an odd mixture of ingredients: scholarship and sentimentalism, erudite quotations and homely phrases, lessons in righteous conduct and suggestions of immoral behavior, melodramatic excitement and tender pathos, characters of worldly sophistication and naive rural people. The author also restricted her technique by giving realism so little opportunity in projecting these materials. Perhaps *St. Elmo* should not be read as a work of art, but rather as a social document from our past.

The popularity of this best seller attracted numerous theatrical producers who were eager to share the profits from a dramatic version of the story, but Mrs. Wilson hesitated to give her permission. It is possible that she suspected that the sensational events in the story, particularly the sentimental scenes, did not miss melodrama very far, and she was afraid of what the actors would do to the story. Numerous critics had recognized *St. Elmo's* kinship with the appeals of popular drama in the day. Miss Evans harbored no Puritanical notions about the evils of the theatre *per se;* rather, she felt that she had a greater obligation to the hundreds of devout readers who sent her letters testifying to the good that this book had done them. She did not wish this favorite story to be "butchered to make a melodrama," as she once put it.

Her old-fashioned publishing firm (now controlled by G. W. Dillingham, who had succeeded Carleton) helped her to guard against dramatization because they believed a theatrical version would injure the steady sales of the book. However, in 1907, two years before her death, Mrs. Wilson relented and gave John P. Ritter permission to copyright a play based on *St. Elmo,* but when the producer presented his final script to her for approval, she refused to allow him to introduce "pickaninnies" and a quartette of colored singers for local realism. Somehow, she believed that such familiar details would not harmonize with the idealistic purposes of the story—that "real life" does not produce an ennobling impression. Similar objections have often cropped up in literary criticism; did not Matthew Arnold find fault with Chaucer's sturdy realism because it lacked "high seriousness"?

Only a few months before Mrs. Wilson's death, Ritter's version was adjusted to suit her taste, but the producer's sentimental plan of exhibiting the play first in Mobile, as a tribute to the novelist, was prevented by her death. From 1909 to about 1915, *St. Elmo* had many successful runs in large and small cities. Within seven years of the date of Ritter's copyright, there were eight additional applications for copyright on plays based on this famous story, and the most popular of all dramatizations of the book, that which Willard Holcomb composed for Vaughn Glaser, was never formally registered with the Library of Congress. Oddly enough, the old story was done over again for the stage as late as the year 1941, when Preston Conway applied for copyright on a "comedy drama" entitled *Saint Elmo.*

The play remained a standard offering in the repertoire of stock companies for many years. It normally was presented in the cheaper houses in Chicago, or New York, or Brooklyn, alternating with such popular favorites as *Uncle Tom's Cabin, The Clansman, Mrs. Wiggs of the Cabbage Patch*, Thurston the Magician, *School*

Days, and Elinor Glyn's *Three Weeks.*[127] The tone of dramatic reviews of *St. Elmo* is somewhat condescending, but the critics were obviously impressed with the play's promise of success with the general public. The leading theatrical journal of the day says of a New York premiere on Christmas Day, 1909: "This is a typical play for the masses. The author, largely in deference to the wishes of Mrs. Evans [sic], who wrote the novel more than a generation ago, has preserved not only the atmosphere but the language of the book, and the characters hold forth in the ceremonious periods of the society of the old South."[128] The critic reminds his reader that the play cannot be enjoyed unless the play-goer has "a capacity to approach it in a spirit of respect for the favorite fiction of our mothers, who wept and thrilled over its pages as they did over those of *Lady Audley's Secret* and *East Lynne.*" Like the stage versions of these novels, *St. Elmo* is likely "to prove a favorite of the masses for years to come. On the stormiest night of the season, there were few vacant seats in the large Academy of Music."

At the dawn of the film industry, Hollywood took notice of *St. Elmo's* box office possibilities. The William Fox Studios released the movie version of the novel in September, 1914. A second photoplay based on *St. Elmo* was released in September, 1923, with the company's outstanding stars in the cast: John Gilbert as St. Elmo, Warner Baxter as Murray Hammond, Bessie Love as Edna Earl, and Barbara LaMarr as Agnes Powell. The studio considered the production a success. It was re-issued in October, 1927, and had another profitable run.[129]

CHAPTER XII

Marriage and Ashland

1868

THE SUCCESS OF *St. Elmo* from the moment of its appearance down to our time has provoked a variety of comment. Some reviewers have said that it was a personal triumph for a clever young moralist. Others have remarked cynically that the "fame" of the book is merely additional evidence that popular taste in literature has been very low in this country. Until recently, only one other woman in our history, Harriett Beecher Stowe, has made such a lasting impression upon the American reading public. And like this scholarly New England lady, Miss Evans was subjected to more stinging abuse than she merited. Perhaps in compensation, the defenders of *St. Elmo* adopted such extravagance in their praise that Miss Evans's head was slightly turned. After hearing remarks like the following, it is understandable that she came to think of her popular success as a subject above criticism, as an honored souvenir of a beloved public: "With a fancy bold and fervid—with an imagination as warm and luxurious as the breath of the orange groves of her own sunny land—with a taste cultivated and refined by a thorough knowledge of classical and modern belles-lettres—with a genius as versatile as DeStael's and as spiritual as Hannah More's—we are ready to crown her Queen Regnant of Southern Literature."[130]

If Miss Evans's ego was somewhat inflated over this success, she did not allow her reputation to alter her homely sense of responsibility for her family, friends and neighbors. During this year of her greatest triumph, she was undoubtedly tempted to carry out her earlier plans to travel widely, possibly to tour Europe. Just after the war, one of her rich New York friends—probably Mrs. J. C. Derby—had invited Augusta "to accompany her to Europe and remain several years, at her expense," but Augusta would not consider leaving her family at that critical time.[131] This invitation had been renewed a year later, when she confided to Curry: "One of the greatest temptations of my life is now set before me: namely, to throw down my pen, leave my works and all our mournful memories behind me, and rest and lose myself among the glories of Europe."[132] Now in the spring and summer of 1867 she had ample funds to satisfy this lifelong desire independently, but she remained at Georgia Cottage where she was needed. Equally tempting was the thought of a triumphant visit to New York, where Mr. Derby would certainly take pleasure in presenting her to society as the most successful author of the day.

Instead of indulging these pleasant fancies, Augusta remained near the bedside of her father, who was now critically ill. Howard Evans had recovered his memory, after the devastating effects of typhoid fever, but his wound had left him permanently lame in one arm.

Both needed her expert services as nurse. There were other pressing obligations at this time which a successful authoress, keenly appreciative of her readers' admiration, was eager to fulfill. She wrote Curry about the hundreds of letters which she had to answer, "letters begging photographs,—autographs,—letters from poor crippled soldiers, asking me to find them employment,—from Episcopal clergymen, requesting me to have them 'called' to some church, and to make up schools for their wives,—letters from young gentlemen at college, praying for lists of books which they should read in conjunction with their textbooks,—and letters plaintive from young ladies who see from the newspapers that I am going to Europe very soon, and are in profound distress, fearing that I may be drowned in crossing the Atlantic Ocean! There is no rest for the wicked!"[133]

A tragic experience of this time, one of the saddest which Augusta ever faced, robbed her of much joy which she might have had in her literary success. Of the many girls named for her, the outstanding favorite was little Augusta Evans, the infant daughter of her brother, Vivian Rutherford Evans. The letters to Curry are filled with expressions of affection for "little Gussie." In January, 1867, Gussie Evans died at age twenty-two months. Augusta wrote Curry that the sorrow was almost more than she could bear. A very tender obituary was written by the novelist and published in one of the Mobile papers; a signed clipping of it was sent to Curry.[134] This was the second name-sake to die in childhood, the first being a little girl in Georgia, whose parents (named Evans, but not relatives) had been so deeply impressed with *Beulah* that they named their child for the author.

Besides her responsibilities at home, there were other requests for her competent aid and advice. Down the highway a quarter-mile from Georgia Cottage was the comfortable estate called Ashland, almost hidden from view by the spreading liveoaks which bordered the private road that led to the Wilson house. Augusta always called at Ashland when she heard that there was illness in the family. Since the fatal illness of the first Mrs. Wilson in 1862, Augusta had been especially helpful, and though the Wilson and Evans families had been friendly neighbors for years, a closer bond developed between them in the middle sixties. Augusta's sense of duty, particularly her response to domestic emergencies, had a binding Puritanical quality which drove her to sacrifice personal desires and comforts when she believed that her services were needed by anyone—relatives, friends or strangers, rich or poor.

The owner of Ashland, Colonel Lorenzo Madison Wilson (the title was honorary, but everyone except Augusta Evans Wilson used it) was sixty years old in 1868, but his lively gait and sparkling eyes were younger than his years. Mr. Wilson made a striking appearance: the hair of his head and brows was very dark, but his beard was gray and his eyes light blue. In spite of the difference in their ages, Augusta and the Colonel had much in common, particularly their love of gardening and animals. Already the flowering shrubs at Ashland were gaining local fame, and possibly the advice of the novelist from Georgia Cottage had much to do with their beauty.

Early in 1868 Augusta and Mr. Wilson realized that they were no longer just neighborly friends, that they had fallen in love. This match probably did not surprise the admirers of *Beulah* and *St. Elmo,* for the heroines of these books were attracted to men much older than themselves. Augusta was thirty-two when they became engaged, and her mental and emotional maturity gave her a warm appreciation of Mr. Wilson's kindliness, courtesy and dignity, as well as the evidences of his complete infatuation for her. Among his fellow businessmen he often boasted that she was not only the greatest woman in America, but also the handsomest and most elegant in her tastes.

It was evident at this time that Mr. Evans might not live long, but Augusta decided that she must tell him about her love for Mr. Wilson, even though she suspected that he would not approve, for the Colonel was four months older than Augusta's father. Matt Evans protested against the marriage as vigorously as his strength would permit, and in deference to his condition Augusta and Mr. Wilson decided to postpone their marriage.

In the summer of 1868 Augusta and her mother were advised to take Mr. Evans to New York, where he could be placed in the care of a specialist. Mr. Wilson used his influence as railroad official to secure special accommodations for the Evans family, but the trip was unsuccessful. On August 27, Matt Evans died on the train en route to Mobile.

In this time of trial Augusta demonstrated the virtues which she so often bestowed upon the heroines of her romances: great common sense, an iron will, competence in emergencies, and resistance to emotional tensions. A weaker woman, particularly in that sentimental age, might have found ample excuse for indulging herself in this period of public and private adulation, intensified by family tragedy. Her idealism, always completely American, was perceived with reference to the practical affairs of the day. And a clear index to her character is exhibited in two decisions: first, that her marriage must take place shortly, in spite of her father's recent death; and second, that her romance must not interfere with her fifth novel, *Vashti,* which was ready for the publisher just six months later!

On the second of December, 1868, Augusta married Lorenzo Madison Wilson in a quiet ceremony at Georgia Cottage. Mr. Wilson, a native of Rock Creek Parish, Maryland, had settled in Mobile in 1831. The size of his patrimony is not known, but his own exertions must have added greatly to his inheritance, for he prospered continuously in the Gulf city. At the time of his marriage to Augusta, Mr. Wilson was an officer and director in the city's leading bank, a director in the Mobile and Montgomery Railroad, and principal stockholder of the street-car line which connected Spring Hill with Mobile. His investments outside the South prevented him from suffering greatly from the defeat of the Confederacy, but his loyalty to the South was undoubtedly above reproach, or such an arch-rebel as Miss 'Gusta Evans would never have accepted him in marriage.

Ashland in 1910

Augusta Evans Wilson in 1903

Colonel L. M. Wilson in 1890

As mistress of spacious Ashland, Augusta Evans Wilson (as she was soon known throughout the land) was faced with several unenviable domestic situations. Mr. Wilson had four living children: Albert, who was twenty-five and married; Mary, twenty-one and married; Louis Madison, whose marriage took place only thirty-four days after his father's, when Madison was only nineteen; and Frances, called Fannie by everyone, who was thirteen. It is a tribute to Augusta's sound judgment that adjustments of these young people to a youthful step-mother were made quickly, without friction. An especially close bond of affection developed between Augusta and teen-age Fannie. The eldest daughter, Mary Wilson Cox, had served as her father's housekeeper for several years after her mother's death, and this circumstance might easily have led to strained feelings, but such did not occur. Perhaps Augusta's experiences as eldest daughter in a large family had prepared her for these delicate adjustments.

Admirers of Mrs. Wilson's books were prepared for her life at Ashland, for most of her heroines, though tested by poverty and adversity, are allowed to wed wealthy men who are accustomed to luxury. All her stories seem to argue that ambitious, Christian girls, whose virtue is attended by circumspection, are justified in expecting material successes as comforting as their spiritual benefits. Rise from poverty to mansion luxury has been the great American story since the appearance of Franklin's *Autobiography,* and the reading public is not likely to tire of it as long as Americans continue to believe that each man of integrity, industry and good luck may yet win his fortune.

Not long after Mrs. Wilson assumed the management of Ashland, this estate became one of the show places of Mobile, and it has remained that down to our time, though it is now a thickly settled residential section. It is now called Ashland Place, and the beauty of its moss-laden liveoaks and flowering shrubbery matches the glowing descriptions written by Mrs. Wilson's visitors—Marse Henry Watterson, J. C. Derby, Louise Manly, LaSalle Corbell Pickett, T. C. DeLeon and other sentimental Victorians. When Augusta was a bride at Ashland, the liveoaks were smaller but they were the special pride of the Wilsons, for the Colonel had planted some of them himself in the late eighteen forties, and their evergreen branches along the driveway to the house always made a lasting impression upon visitors. Possibly other relics of the earlier time are still there—magnolias and cedars, perhaps a few hardy azaleas and camellia-japonicas which Mrs. Wilson and the Colonel attended. But the house at the end of the drive was destroyed by fire in 1926.

Ashland is three miles west of the business district, on Springhill Avenue, just opposite the Convent of the Visitation. Colonel Wilson bought the forty acres of land in 1844 and built the house for his first wife, who was Sarah Ann Chandler. Architects usually refer to the Wilson house as "Greek revival," but the structure was not as imposing as this name suggests. Mobilians often apply the simple name of "raised cottage" to this style of house. The principal entrances to the house at Ashland were on the second floor, and the ground floor was used mainly for kitchen needs and storage. The house had identical facades in the front and rear, one facing Springhill Avenue and the other Old Shell Road. Each entrance was dominated by a row of six fluted columns which extended from the ground to the roof, beyond which was a spacious veranda. The main floor contained eight large rooms, besides a wide hall which connected the two entrances. This hall was the brightest and coolest part of the house, and it was here that Augusta soon established her study and began work upon *Vashti.* There were many handsome antiques at Ashland which had belonged to the first Mrs. Wilson, but Augusta selected a few new pieces for her living room and study which were more notable for comfort and sturdiness than for their antiquity.

Long before the establishment of Mobile's colorful Azalea Trail, the Wilson shrubs were famous locally. Many new varieties of camellia-japonicas were developed by the novelist, and one of them is so unusual that modern fanciers often doubt its existence: the unique quality of this camellia is that it has a scent, a factor almost unknown in other varieties of the plant; its blossom is the double type, pink in shade, with many folding petals. Cuttings from this famous shrub were rooted by Mrs. L. M. Wilson, Jr., and one of the plants was set out at the home of Maddie Wilson, who became Mrs. S. Palmer Gaillard in 1893. Miss Mary Gaillard, Maddie's daughter, says that the odor is very faint today, but it must have been stronger in the youth of the species, for numerous people have testified as to its fragrance, among them was the Atlanta author, Lollie Belle Wylie.[135] The Gaillards gave this camellia the name of "Augusta Evans Wilson," and it is advertised by this name in the catalogs of the Overlook Nursery, who obtained cuttings from the Gaillards. Floral designs composed of this flower and other rare specimens from Ashland were sensational hits on several public occasions.

Besides the remarkable winter blooming azaleas and camellias—which were not as widely popular then as now—Ashland was famous for its maidenhair ferns and imported tulips of unique size and color, its hundreds of white Roman hyacinths and many varieties of roses, geraniums and begonias. Mrs. Wilson gave all of them her personal attention, supervising the removal of plants from flower-beds or verandas to hot-houses as the seasons changed. At one time, the grounds at Ashland contained five hot-houses (Southerners have never preferred the term "greenhouse"). One was filled with every known species of fish geranium, another with a miscellaneous collection of potted plants, and the other three with different varieties of camellias. Fanciers of japonicas in that day usually protected them in winter or kept them in a hot-house the year round.

The acres of grounds contained other picturesque sights. Many varieties of fowls were allowed to graze on the lawns and under the chinaberry trees and Japanese quince. Every domestic bird was snow-white, because the Wilsons thought that the white figures of turkeys, geese, leghorns and guinea-fowl made a pretty sight when set off against a background of green.

Augusta's varied interests and constant activity demonstrated that she had learned early in life to budget her time. This trait is mentioned frequently by her friends and relatives, one of whom remarked that the affairs at Ashland were conducted on such a strict schedule that a neighbor could tell the time of day by the chore which a Wilson servant was performing. "In her household management," recalled Mrs. L. M. Wilson, Jr., "Mammie was very systematic. She had certain days set aside for everything. Her servants may have thought her a little hard, although they were all loyal and loved her. However, she was exacting and made them do everything perfectly. If they broke a dish, she sent them to town to replace it from their own earnings. Naturally, the servants didn't make dish-breaking a pastime. She would always make up to them by giving them something they needed for the money they spent in replacing broken dishes."[136]

Mrs. Wilson's treatment of servants was often praised by callers. In giving orders to Fannie or Jerry she invariably added "please," and she took pains to thank them for their services. The long tenure of her servants, even in the critical Reconstruction period, was mentioned by many friends.

Jerry Miles, the yard boy who married Fannie Lewis, the housemaid, was once called into court as a witness in a damage suit. The opposing counsel asked him, "Didn't you live on the place of Mrs. Bragg's sister, Mrs. Wilson?" Jerry answered with enthusiasm, "Yassir, me and Miss 'Gusta lived together forty years." He was Mr. Wilson's man before the novelist came to Ashland,

and he was still in Mrs. Wilson's employ at the time of her death in 1909.

Efficient housekeeping was a fitting supplement to Mrs. Wilson's literary career, neither of which appeared to interfere with the other; in fact, Mrs. Wilson was an early advocate of dignified careers for women, *provided* the women did not neglect the domestic responsibilities which society and nature expected of them. Nearly every book which she published contains attacks upon selfish women or fashionable matrons who fail to respond to their household duties. She even blames them for many a wayward daughter, dissipated son, or drunken husband.

At Ashland the day started early. Before dawn the yard boy prepared the fire in the kitchen stove for the cook, Aunt Ann, who busied herself with a chore which became one of Ashland's noteworthy traditions: hot beaten biscuits for breakfast. This Southern delicacy—a crisp, dry, unsweetened but very tasteful small biscuit—requires at least an hour to prepare. Aunt Ann laid out her biscuit dough on a large section of tree trunk which was cut for this purpose; with a stout pestle shaped like a baseball bat, she beat the dough thoroughly. The Ashland beaten biscuits had their own distinct label: a dotted cross which was made with a child's fork. In spite of their tedious preparation, fresh beaten biscuits were served each morning, a custom which was continued until Mrs. Wilson's death.

Another pleasant custom in this gracious household was the placing of a flower beside the master's breakfast plate; Mr. Wilson's napkin ring had a small hand in which a sprig of clematis (his favorite flower) or a camellia could be inserted, a chore performed regularly by Mrs. Wilson during their twenty-three years of married life. After breakfast she pinned the flower to the Colonel's lapel, and then they took their daily stroll through the gardens, hot-houses and dairy barns. Orders were given in Mr. Wilson's presence so that he could make his own suggestions. In good weather their tour of the place ended with a walk down the arcade of liveoaks to the gate on Springhill Avenue. Here he usually found a dummy-car awaiting him, one of the horse-drawn street cars which were operated by his traction company. Augusta awaited the departure of the car, waved to Mr. Wilson (as she normally called him), and returned to her well planned routine in the house. Most certainly she did not throw him a kiss in parting—as one sentimental reminiscence has her doing—for such conduct in public was foreign to her nature.

Augusta Evans Wilson's appearance was probably not so arresting as her husband's, in spite of the difference in their ages, but her face was remarkable for one feature which contemporaries were too reticent to describe: her eyes were polychromatic, one blue and one brown. Her normal expression was quite serious—some called it sharp—but her features broke easily into a smile. Her deepest pleasure was exhibited with a twinkle about her eyes, the rest of her face remaining immobile. Her dignity in public, the elegance of her manners, and her sensible though firm endeavors to maintain her privacy at Ashland were probably responsible for the impression which she often made upon strangers—of sternness and too great independence of will. She was unquestionably a strong-minded woman who attacked sin and follies with a stubborn zeal, and she was often impatient with people who wasted her time and theirs, but friends and relatives recall many evidences of a gentleness which stood in contrast to her stony will.

All the inmates of Ashland were familiar with her fondness for nicknames and her love of teasing. Perhaps there is no clearer indication of her common sense and good humor than the forbearance with which she accepted the atrocious nicknames applied to her. When the Colonel's grandchild, little Maddie Wilson, came to Ashland to live, someone taught her to call the novelist "Mammie," an appellation which seemed to please Mrs. Wilson. All the servants at Ashland—in fact everyone except Mr. Wilson and his daughter Fannie—normally called her "Miss 'Gusta," and though Mrs. Wilson protested good-naturedly throughout her life, she never tried seriously to end the practice. Such gentle humanity helps to mollify the impression that she was too often headstrong, efficient and cold. The record of her life at Georgia Cottage and at Ashland suggests that she knew how to win affection from many types of people.

She reciprocated in the matter of nicknames by calling her dignified husband "Junebug," and by addressing children affectionately as "Chicken." She teased the Colonel about his hobbies—horse racing and cock fighting—but there is no evidence that she wanted him to drop them. She might say that the walls of her dining room had "so many pictures of thoroughbreds that the room looked like a livery stable," but she never replaced them. If the Colonel requested that only eggs newly laid be served for his breakfast, or that only butter newly churned be served with his hot beaten biscuits, she might laugh and complain mildly, but these little preferences of her husband were satisfied every day in the year. Another stimulant to good-natured teasing was Mr. Wilson's boyish resistance to church going. His excuses were as varied and subtle as Mark Twain's, but the one which gave Mrs. Wilson most trouble was his complaint of poor health once or twice a month, but invariably on Sunday. She used to laugh and say that Mr. Wilson took his pills on Saturday just so he could avoid church the next day.

The morning routine at Ashland, after the master's departure, consisted first of the careful planning of the dinner meal, which was served soon after Mr. Wilson's return in the late afternoon. There were certain prescribed menus and recipes, the product of years of gracious living, and the servants were trained to prepare the dishes which complemented each other, but Mrs. Wilson admitted that she could contribute little to kitchen techniques. Aunt Ann knew the exact time each day when she was expected to present her plans for dinner, and the arrangements were just as elaborate for the immediate family as for guests. The grace which was said at Ashland was always the Lord's Prayer. Augusta seldom introduced her literary interests into the conversation, unless Mr. Wilson indicated that he was eager to hear about her writing or reading. He had great esteem for her literary accomplishments, and undoubtedly liked to hear his gifted wife discuss her books, but Augusta's instinct for good talk told her when to begin or cease.

When arrangements for dinner were complete, Mrs. Wilson opened her writing desk. Before taking up the manuscript of her latest novel, she answered all business and personal letters, usually on the day that each was received. Her correspondence was done in her own elegant handwriting until late in life, when Howard Evans assumed this responsibility for her.

Shortly before her marriage, Augusta joined the St. Francis Street Methodist Church and became a member of its choir, where she sang each Sunday for the next twenty-five years. On week-days she set aside a few minutes for the rehearsal of numbers for the coming service; at first, she was dependent upon Mary Wilson or Mrs. Madison Wilson to accompany her on the organ, but later she learned to play a little herself. At an earlier period she picked the guitar as an accompaniment to her singing. Her strong soprano voice was much admired from the choir, but the family servants probably had other opinions of her daily singing. One relative remembers that an old servant, an ex-slave of the family, remarked one day, "My Lawd, Miss 'Gusta sounds like a howling hound dog!"

One duty which she enjoyed particularly was a daily visit to her mother, who still lived at Georgia Cottage. In bad weather, Uncle Jerry had the carriage ready just after lunch for this visit, but Augusta usually walked the quarter-mile up Springhill Avenue. Unlike many

Southern belles and matrons, she had never been afraid of exercise, even in the warm afternoons.

Augusta's deep affection for her mother has been mentioned before. Her royalties from novels had always been shared with the family, but perhaps the most striking instance of her generosity to Mrs. Evans is seen in her gift of a check for $15,000 the year following her marriage. This check, which we shall hear more about later, was the publisher's initial payment for *Vashti.*

The best record of Augusta's personality is certainly to be found in her books and in her deeds, but numerous visitors and friends printed their impressions of her character, a few of whom indulged in uncomplimentary gossip about her sternness and sharp tongue. One of the unique character-studies of her was written by James Wood Davidson, whose history of Southern literature appeared in 1869. Although Davidson's sketch of Mrs. Wilson is based upon her penmanship and several letters, his judgment of her character corresponds with numerous isolated remarks about her: "[Mrs. Wilson's penmanship] has a look both elaborate and emphatic. It reveals even more character than her person does; indicating the cultivated woman of will, system, clearness, and energy of thought; a perseverance—we are tempted to say persistence—rare in woman; a steadiness and remarkable uniformity of manner; an absence of all levity; with some fondness for display and *eclat* . . . [Her handwriting] conveys the idea of practicalness rather than of sentiment or ornament; and this we may take to be true as applied to herself."[137]

A few popular prejudices of the time were shared by Mrs. Wilson, but she had no patience with the puritanical attacks upon the theatre, often repeated then as now. Mobile was undoubtedly more liberal in this respect than many other small American cities, for the theatre had flourished there since early in the century. Edwin Booth, John McCullough, and other stars of the day had regular engagements in Mobile. On one occasion Mrs. Wilson sent word to McCullough that she would be glad to receive him at Ashland. The great Shakespearean actor must have felt honored to receive a summons from the successful novelist, for he immediately arranged an afternoon appointment. Mrs. Wilson was pleased that he came out to Ashland alone; she had previously decided that she did not want to share the interview with others. They talked for a while about Shakespeare and about McCullough's interpretations of famous passages, and as their enthusiasm mounted, the great actor constantly jumped to his feet and recited memorable lines just as he delivered them from the stage. It was a period of grandiose acting—with sweeping gestures and solemn pantomime, elegant articulations and intonations. In later years Mrs. Wilson took much pleasure in recalling this exciting afternoon with the famous tragedian who performed grandiloquently for his audience of one.

Her reward for this special performance was also unique. During the intermission at McCullough's next presentation of *Virginius,* he stood at the footlights to receive the floral tributes which wealthy patrons customarily bestowed upon famous stars. This night the actor was to receive one which took his breath: a liveried messenger came down the aisle with a design in the form of a large Roman shield, its background of snow-white camellias with a royal purple border of violets. Diagonally across the white field was a crimson dagger of red geraniums. McCullough placed the huge offering before the footlights, read aloud the attached card, and amidst the applause of a partisan audience, he walked across the stage to the Wilson box and thanked the novelist with his most graceful bow. A commercial florist had assembled the unique favor according to Mrs. Wilson's instructions, but the flowers came from her own hot-houses.[138]

Augusta's only experience in dramatics was a notable local success. She persuaded Mobile's young social set to coöperate fully in an ambitious undertaking: the production of the Oriental romance, *Lalla Rookh,* for the benefit of the Protestant Orphan Asylum. Under Augusta's direction, the rehearsals went off smoothly and the rich custumes were designed and tailored. The performance was a spectacular success, particularly the work of the young dancing girls, whose grace and charm owed much to the director.[139]

Augusta's liberal views on the theatre were matched by her unusual stand on prohibition—also more characteristic of Mobile than of many other Southern cities. She deplored intemperance in any form, but she could not share the contemporary reformers' zeal for abstinence, and she was sure that moral values could not be legislated into people. Many of her guests at Ashland recorded their delight in the fine scuppernong wine which she made herself, squeezing each grape between two fingers. The wine was corked early enough in its fermentation to produce an effervescence similar to that of champagne. When stimulants were served at her table, she sipped a little from her own glass so that the guests would feel free to partake as they chose, but wine did not agree with her, even her own clear, beaded scuppernong.

Mrs. Wilson's stand on prohibition was allied to her position on woman's suffrage, for many suffragettes took an active part in the prohibition movement. She believed that woman's place in the home is so important that she should not lower herself in public estimation by campaigning for this reform. She shared the popular prejudice of the time that politics at best was slightly degrading, and that the noisy women reformers were not a credit to their sex. One who knew her well has written that she "could not tolerate any deviation from the oldtime ideal of womanhood . . . She could not bring her mind to accept the spectacle of women forcing legislation by demonstrations at the polls and in the halls of the legislature. During the height of the prohibition fight, Mrs. Wilson coined the saying, 'If women attended to their privileges, they would not need to be keen about their rights.' "[140]

Mrs. Wilson was sceptical of all organizations which might lessen woman's influence in the home. She made no exception of women's clubs and patriotic societies. Invitations to speak before them were tactfully but briefly refused, and her answers to inquiries about relatives who served in the Revolution or in the War Be-

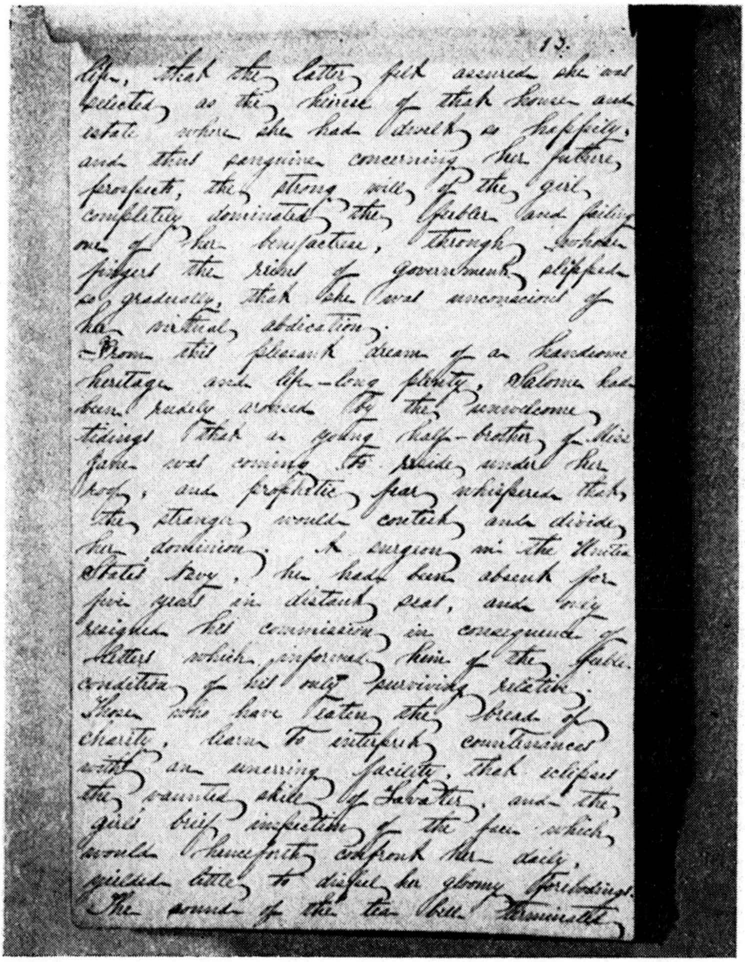

13.

life, that the latter felt assured she was selected as the heiress of that house and estate where she had dwelt so happily, and thus sanguine concerning her future prospects, the strong will of the girl completely dominated the feebler and failing one of her benefactress, through whose fingers the reins of government slipped so gradually, that she was unconscious of her virtual abdication.

From this pleasant dream of a handsome heritage and life-long plenty, Salome had been rudely aroused by the unwelcome tidings that a young half-brother of Miss Jane was coming to reside under her roof, and prophetic fear whispered that the stranger would contest and divide her dominion. A surgeon in the United States Navy, he had been absent for five years in distant seas, and only resigned his commission in consequence of letters which informed him of the feeble condition of his only surviving relative.

Those who have eaten the bread of charity, learn to interpret countenances with an unerring facility, that eclipses the vaunted skill of Lavater, and the girl's brief inspection of the face which would henceforth confront her daily, yielded little to dispel her gloomy forebodings.

The sound of the tea bell terminated

A Page from the Manuscript of Vashti

Photograph of Mrs. Wilson, Used in Promoting A Speckled Bird

tween the States usually contained only a few polite notes about verifiable names and dates. She honored tradition but she was too modest to advertise her family's place in it. As for social clubs, she thought most of them were a waste of time, which could better be spent with household duties or in cultivating one's mind.

CHAPTER XIII

Vashti

1869-1875

MOST WOMEN of normal energies and interests would consider the management of Ashland, with its accompanying social and religious responsibilities, to be a full-time vocation, but Augusta was an exceptional woman. Although the new adjustments which were required of her at Ashland placed a limitation upon her pursuit of literary and scholarly interests, she did not allow domestic matters to interfere with her schedule of four hours each weekday at her writing desk. She was determined that her fifth novel should be the instrument of as much good as possible, though it would be a publishing miracle if *Vashti* were read by as many people as read *St. Elmo.* The prestige of her recent best seller, particularly its reputation as a moving moral document, had appealed to a vast reading public, and her publisher was making inquiries about the progress of her work.

Finally, when George W. Carleton read the manuscript, he began immediate negotiations with Mrs. Wilson to purchase all rights to *Vashti,* and he was willing to risk a considerable sum (for that day) on its saleability. They agreed upon $15,000, payable in advance of publication, for all copyright privileges, a sum which must be multiplied several times if we are to view it in terms of the "reconstructed" South of 1869. Colonel Wilson, a successful capitalist in his own right, was particularly pleased with his wife's earning power.

Mrs. Wilson's business relations with her publishers were unique throughout her long career. We have followed Derby's and Lippincott's unselfish acts in her behalf, and G. W. Carleton was equally generous. The shrewd publisher knew that *Vashti* was a fairly safe risk, even at $15,000, but he was amazed at the profits which this book earned. No steps were taken by Mrs. Wilson to have the contract reconsidered; she was content with the initial payment. However, the profits from the venture were so much more than Carleton had estimated that he willingly tore up his first contract and returned the copyright to the author. Though not legally bound to do so, Carleton paid her semi-annual royalties on *Vashti* for many years.[141] Such fairness and altruism in a commercial relationship was deeply appreciated by Mrs. Wilson, who remained staunchly loyal to this firm until her death.

Thomas C. DeLeon states that a rival publisher once sent an agent to Mobile with an offer of $25,000 for permission to issue cheap editions of her books, but Mrs. Wilson refused it on the grounds that such a plan would not be fair to the original publisher who had been willing to take the first risk.[142] She received scores of handsome offers from magazines for stories, but she rejected all of them with the argument that she had a publisher who was eager to bring out anything she might care to write. The greater profits from magazine publication, plus later issue in book form, did not appeal to her as highly as the good will of her publisher. It is no wonder that Derby, Carleton, Dillingham (who controlled the same firm in succession), and their friendly rival, Lippincott, had such high regard for their loyal author and friend down in Mobile.

The Colonel's business acumen was excited by the striking evidence of his bride's prestige and earning power. He carried the $15,000 check in his pocket so that he could display it before his friends downtown. When Augusta decided to bestow the full sum upon her mother, Mr. Wilson reluctantly deposited the check in her name, but not before he had secured a facsimile print of it.

A large portion of the readers who awaited Mrs. Wilson's next book had been attracted by the "message" of *St. Elmo*—a fervent sermon on the manner in which a dissolute rake is converted through the ministry of a Christian girl. Books containing such moral and religious appeals have always dominated our best seller lists—*Uncle Tom's Cabin, St. Elmo, Barriers Burned Away, Ben-Hur, In His Steps,* and even in our sophisticated time, *The Magnificent Obsession* and *The Robe.* Their authors have not only been rewarded richly in financial returns, but thousands of readers have addressed confidential letters to them about the good which their stories have done.

Vashti; or, Until Death Us Do Part was composed for such earnest people and for others who respected or needed Christian principles. The sub-title indicates that the author will treat some aspect of marriage. The chief target is divorce, which is constantly assailed in ringing italics: *"Human legislation is impotent to cancel the statutes of Almighty God, which declare that only death can free what Jehovah has joined together."*

The old character-types of the earlier novels reappear: the flawless, intellectual heroine; the dignified, scholarly hero; and the ambitious, artistic female orphan. As in *St. Elmo,* there is a profusion of erudite references and quotations; scholarly discussions of literature or of painting frequently introduce the sentimental conversations. In one representative purple passage, the heroine remembers the grievous wrong she has suffered as the result of a loveless marriage; and like Hamlet she soliloquizes upon suicide in the grand manner:

> *Au pis aller,* if the burden of life becomes utterly intolerable I can shuffle it off as quickly as did that proud Roman, who "when the birds began to sing" in the dawn of a day heralded by tempestuous winds laden with perfume from the vales of Sicily, shut his eyes forever from the warm sparkling Mediterranean billows that broke in the roads of Utica, and pricked the memory of inattentive Azrael with the point of a sword. Neither Phaedo, family, nor fame, could coax Cato to respect the prerogative of Atropos; and if he, "the only free and unconquered man," quailed and fled before the apparition of numerous advancing years, what marvel that I, who am neither sage nor Roman, should be tempted some fine morning when the birds are sounding reveille around my chamber windows, to imitate "what Cato did, and Addison approved."

The reviewers once again had a field day with Mrs. Wilson's style. A critic in New Orleans concludes his attack upon the book: "*Vashti* may therefore be safely pronounced a case of affectation run mad, in which the dictionary has been ruthlessly plundered of its unused treasures in order to astound the public."[143] Her answer to such abuse is deftly expressed in the preface to her next novel, *Infelice* (1875), when she quotes from Disraeli's *Lothair*: "Tomorrow the critics will commence. You know who the critics are? The men who have failed in literature and art." Not a kind retort from one who averaged about $10,000 a year from her royalties between 1870 and 1900, though she published only two new books in that period. Her unkindness, however, was mild compared to the savagery of her critics.

When one considers the constant repetition of excesses in her books—quotations, abstruse references, pompous scholarly terms—all of which produced a continuous storm of protest from the critics, one naturally suspects that Mrs. Wilson had a subtle motive in using such an exotic style. Several accuse her of seeking their abuse for its advertising value. Davidson, writing in 1869, said that her pedantry was "well calculated to excite the unmeasured spite" of reviewers.[144] A critic for the Montgomery *Advertiser* said in 1887: "We have a notion that her abomination of big words and unnatural conversations and people were purposely adopted by a woman who must sell her books, and knew the quickest way was to provoke the critics."[145] Augusta did not choose to answer this type of argument.

Like most writers of the century, she adorned her story with the "finest" poetic sentiment of our language. The narrative of *Vashti* is interrupted over a hundred times for such passages as the following:

> But when the quivering lips of one breathed a petition before the throne of God, the beautiful cold mouth of the other was muttering bitterly:
>
> "Yea, love is dead, and by her funeral bier
> Ambition gnaws the lips, and sheds no tear;
> And, in the outer chamber Hope sits wild,—
> Hope, with her blue eyes dim with looking long."

Much of her poetic plunder is taken from the journalistic verse of the day, or from the writings of such popular versifiers as Jean Ingelow or Owen Meredith, but occasionally she calls upon Shakespeare, Cowper, Wordsworth, Tennyson, or Mrs. Browning to heighten the emotion of a passage.

As in *Beulah, Macaria* and *St. Elmo,* the lovers in *Vashti* are kept apart for long periods. In this case the heroine is constrained to isolate herself from all normal contacts because of a secret sorrow in her earlier life, a misfortune so grave that her hair turned white in a day. The nature of her tragedy is not revealed for many chapters but at last we are informed that she is "separated" from a degenerate husband who married her for gold. Divorce is out of the question. She is a defeated woman and can only await release from a hateful existence. When death finally comes to Vashti, we are left to believe that she has died of a broken heart.

On finishing the first draft of this sad moral tale, Mrs. Wilson made one of the most remarkable transcriptions ever presented to a typesetter. Her handwriting had always been childishly perfect, with shadings and ornamental dashes, but with this manuscript she outdid herself. It is said that her longhand copy contains no misspellings or discernible erasures. When she was ready to dispatch it to the publisher, her husband requested Carleton to give him the manuscript when the printing was completed. Mr. Wilson had the sheets bound in leather, and he proudly displayed the volume on many occasions. This unique copy is now owned by Mr. Starr Kealhofer, Sr., of Austin, Texas, the grandson of Augusta's sister, Mrs. Sarah Evans Bush, who inherited Augusta's library. Mr. Kealhofer often exhibits it in libraries or at fairs, where it invariably attracts many people.

Vashti has never rivaled *St. Elmo, Tiberius* or *A Speckled Bird* in general popularity, but the publishers have always kept an edition in print. One playwright, Ullie Akerstrom, copyrighted a dramatic version of the novel in 1910, but no record of a performance has been found. Every year or so one meets some evidence of *Vashti's* influence: a woman who was given the rare name of the sombre heroine, or a champion greyhound or a fictional town named Vashti.

DeLeon published an odd anecdote concerning the widespread distribution of Mrs. Wilson's books. He reports that a "quaint international postal card" was mailed to the author from Agra, India, by her publisher, George W. Carleton, who informed her: "Will you believe me when I tell you . . . that today I saw a Parsee boy reading a London edition of *Vashti*—here—here! miles and miles up the jungles of interior India—within a stone's throw of the amazingly beautiful Taj

Mahal, surrounded by magnificent, half-ruined palaces, tombs and temples, barbaric mosques, wild monkeys and venomous snakes, turbaned Mohammedans and naked Hindoos . . ."[146]

By the year 1870, Mrs. Wilson's health began to suffer from the strain of her many interests. Writing, study, housekeeping, singing—any one of which was a career in itself—were pursued simultaneously, until Mr. Wilson spoke his mind. The novelist had a will of her own, but her respect for her husband was just as firm. She acceded to his wishes and spent fewer hours at her writing desk and in the library. Instead of attending the sick herself, she considered means of encouraging young girls to take up nursing as a career. A few years later she took an active part in the founding of the Nonsectarian Infirmary in Mobile; she contributed $300 toward the purchase of a site, and in her will she left the hospital, as yet unbuilt, a bequest.

Attacks of insomnia had troubled Augusta since the early days of her authorship, but her most grievous malady was hay fever. During the war she wrote Rachel Lyons that her suffering had driven her from handkerchiefs to towels and that she feared she would have to resort to sheets. For many years, she and Mr. Wilson traveled extensively over the country in search of a climate which would bring relief. At one time she thought that Long Island was the place. The discovery pleased her very much because her sister, Mary Eliza, who became Mrs. Leo Tarleton, lived in New York City, and her good friend Frank Armstrong Crawford, now Mrs. Cornelius Vanderbilt, had several residences in the area. Her enthusiasm for New York was shortlived, for the dreaded attacks recurred there also. She always attributed her allergy (though she did not use that modern term for her sensitiveness) to newly mowed grass or hay, but she never discovered a satisfactory treatment.

In July, 1871, the Wilson and Bragg families were saddened by a tragic death which resulted from an absurd quarrel. Young Braxton Bragg, namesake and nephew of the famous Confederate general, was a suitor of Virginia Evans, a younger sister of the novelist, but he did not allow this fact to restrain him from publishing a letter in a local newspaper criticising the service on Colonel Wilson's Spring Hill Railroad. Mr. Bragg charged that the mules which pulled the dummy were often unhitched at the end of the line, near the gate to Ashland, and used to plow the Colonel's fields. Because of this practice, he charged, the animals were so overworked that they could not draw the cars at a satisfactory speed. The Wilsons naturally resented the letter, particularly young Madison Wilson, who was about the age of Braxton Bragg. There was considerable public discussion of Braxton's letter, and the *Register* published several letters in support of the company and its president. The quarrel grew, and reports reached Braxton that Madison had threatened him. Both young men began to carry pistols.

On the morning of July 8, 1871, the quarrel came to a climax. Braxton Bragg stood on the busiest corner of Mobile, on St. Francis Street by the Customhouse, and awaited the arrival of Madison Wilson, who had let it be known that he was coming to town on the dummy to "see" Braxton. When Madison descended from the car, shots were fired, and Madison suffered a fatal wound. At the preliminary hearing on July 15, Braxton was released on his own recognisance, with the low bail of $2,500. During the hearing the presiding officer stated that "if the defendant could be convicted of any offense, it would be for a minor grade of manslaughter."[147] No indictment was ever brought against Braxton, and apparently public opinion in Mobile did not censure him severely for the tragedy, because he was elected city attorney a few years later, which office he held at the time of his early death.

The newspaper coverage of this shooting offers a revealing sidelight of the times. Because of the prominence of the families and the personal nature of the quarrel, the *Register* reported the incident in two short paragraphs on July 9, giving no details concerning the cause of the quarrel. This unique sentence concludes the brief notice: "We refrain from saying anything further until all the facts are brought out in the trial." The incident was not mentioned again until the hearing, which was summarized with conscious objectivity, and no particulars of the quarrel were ever published.

Feelings within the Wilson family were complicated by the fact that Braxton Bragg was engaged to Mrs. Wilson's sister. The novelist had sided with her husband and stepson in the early stages of the quarrel, and after Madison's death she remained quite bitter toward Mr. Bragg. She naturally opposed Virginia's marriage to him, but her devotion to her sister was so great that she decided to take no action that might bring further unhappiness to Virginia. After the marriage, Mrs. Wilson continued to visit the Braggs very often, and during her last years she was closer to Mrs. Bragg and her four children than to anyone except Howard Evans.

Shortly after the sudden death of Madison Wilson, the novelist arranged to have his widow and infant daughter come to Ashland to live. The child was named for her father, but everyone called her Maddie. A very close bond of affection developed between Augusta and the three feminine members of the household: Mrs. Madison Wilson (called Mollie), Miss Fannie Wilson (seventeen years of age in 1871) and little Maddie. One of the first words which Maddie learned was "Mammie," the name she used for her noted step-grandmother throughout her life.

A charming little diary of Maddie's, for the year 1880 (when she was nine), is now in the possession of her daughter, Miss Mary Gaillard of Mobile. Some of the child's entries give us an insight into the gentler side of the novelist's household, and help to soften the impression of efficiency and discipline which visitors often gained. On August 26 Maddie records, "This morning Mamma [her mother] and Aunt Fannie went over to Mrs. Rickarby's to spend the day. I did not go because I was not invited but I believe Mammie and I had a better time than they did. I read to Mammie and she read to me. She read me a story called 'The Pied Piper of Hamlin.'" At another time Maddie reveals the pleasure she had in helping Mammie pack a box of flowers for Mrs. Cornelius Vanderbilt.

CHAPTER XIV

Infelice and Tiberius

1875-1887

VISITORS in Mobile, particularly the delegates to conventions, were always eager to see the estate of Alabama's best known author. Mrs. Wilson sometimes complained about this intrusion upon her privacy, once remarking that she felt like "a two-headed calf at a circus sideshow," but she usually responded graciously to the demands of these strangers.

Her friends and local visitors were received on Saturday afternoons, although she never admitted that she had a special day to be "at home." Most prominent families in Mobile at this time did observe designated days for receiving callers: Government Street had Tuesdays, and the northern part of town had Thursdays. Mrs. Wilson preferred Saturday because the Colonel returned to Ashland early on this day. These receptions were often quite informal, at least at Ashland. Several visitors recalled that Mr. and Mrs. Wilson wore comfortable "home clothes" on Saturdays.

One amusing incident of a visit by a group of convention delegates was often repeated by Mrs. Wilson. The callers knocked at the door and explained to Melinda, the servant, that they were eager to meet the novelist and to see her flowers. From her writing desk Mrs. Wilson directed Melinda to tell them that she was unable to see them at that time, but that they were welcome to see the place under the maid's direction. She added that Melinda was to give them flowers when they were ready to go. The maid protested that her mistress should receive them because they had come from a great distance, but Mrs. Wilson repeated her original order. When the visitors had departed, Melinda returned to the study and muttered poutingly, "They sho did ask a lot of questions." When she had Mrs. Wilson's attention, she added, "Miss 'Gusta, folks what don't know you thinks you're an angel!"

One famous visitor was "Marse Henry" Watterson, the colorful Louisville editor and author, who made a special pilgrimage to Ashland in the eighties for the purpose of renewing his friendship with Augusta, whom he had met when he was a soldier in gray at Camp Beulah. Both were famous now, and Marse Henry wanted to assure her that he had esteemed her writing and war services just as highly in the old days as he did at the time of her national success. Augusta's friend, Thomas C. DeLeon, took the editor out to Ashland "behind a fast mare," as he later described the visit, and while they talked, Watterson indicated that he stood in awe of Mrs. Wilson's famous name and her reputation for scholarly conversation. Marse Henry was a noted figure himself, but as homespun in speech and as earthy in humor as the great Mark Twain, with whom he was often compared.

When the editor and the novelist met, DeLeon did

not think of introducing them because they were supposed to know each other; however, it had been over twenty years since the war days, and Watterson did not recognize the modest woman before him, whose house dress made her look older than her years. She talked about simple things—"her chickens, flowers, anything but literature"—until Marse Henry became a little restless in his anxiety. He sidled over to DeLeon, put his hand over his lips and said in a low but audible voice, "Say, I wonder if the old lady would send up and tell Miss 'Gusta we are waiting." After the hostess's identity was tactfully made known to him, Marse Henry no longer worried about the lady's impressive scholarship and reputation.[148]

Numerous visitors at Ashland returned to their homes in St. Louis or Louisville or Chicago or New York and wrote glowing accounts of their interviews for local newspapers. All had the same memories of the spacious mansion and its hostess. They were impressed by the "well kept driveway" and the "prettiest lawn [they] had ever seen," which lay beneath the "grand and majestic old live-oaks." They were "ushered into the parlor by an old-time negress in regulation bandana headgear," where they were met by the "distingushed authoress in the hospitable style of the true Southern home," each receiving a handshake ("after the Southern fashion"). She was "neatly clad in pretty gingham costume, and her welcome made all forgetful of formality." She "lived and moved in a vast bower of flowers, all planted and nursed by her own hands, and she exhibited them with all the pride and affection of a

Roman mother." At this time, Mrs. Wilson's hair was "turning slightly gray" and was covered "with a piece of soft old lace, much after the manner seen in the familiar portraits of George Eliot." Her temperament conveyed "nothing of the grand dame or the blue stocking," and her conversation was conducted in simple words—just the opposite to the ostentatious dialogue of her novels. Refreshments were served, of beaten biscuits and "scuppernong wine made by her own hands." The picture which one carried away of this old-fashioned lady was "that of refined and delicate features set in a frame of soft brown curls falling to the shoulders; . . . pleasant expressive eyes, a figure hardly up to medium size, and a delicate appearance, as if the mental structure rather over-balanced the physical."[149]

One notable visitor in Mobile whom Mrs. Wilson would not receive was Oscar Wilde, the English playwright who managed to attract so much gossip to his personal life. Thomas DeLeon had a business interest in the lecture tour of the sensational Englishman, and DeLeon was eager to present Wilde at Ashland. Mrs. Wilson refused bluntly, informing her friend that Wilde's life "defamed his art."[150]

Up to 1869 Augusta's novels had appeared at intervals of less than three years, but her health had been injured by the strain of her varied interests. She tried to follow the Colonel's wishes and work more leisurely upon her sixth novel, *Infelice,* but again she often overtaxed her strength. In spite of her busy routine, she reserved some of her time for the young people at Ashland and for her green-houses and her husband's business affairs. During the early seventies Fannie Wilson was rapidly growing into young womanhood and needed more of her stepmother's attention. Mrs. Madison (Mollie) Wilson and her daughter Maddie were close to the novelist, who shared her valuable time with them and assured them by wise and tactful treatment that Ashland would always be their home. Almost every season of the year found house guests at the estate: the children and grandchildren of the Colonel's first marriage, or Augusta's brothers and sisters with their children.

Mr. Wilson's business interests were expanding in the seventies, and a dutiful wife could not choose but hear about them and share the necessary anxieties. With respect to the Colonel's rowdy hobbies—horse racing and cock fighting—Augusta might grumble occasionally about the frequent trips to his stables in St. Louis or about the crowing of the lusty gamecocks, but she apparently decided that it would be wise to accept her vigorous if elderly husband as he was. She had a great fondness for livestock, as evidenced by her interest in Mr. Wilson's prize cattle; several pictures of these blue-ribboned champions, proudly posed on the lawns at Ashland, are still kept by the great grandchildren.

The Colonel had kept fighting gamecocks at Ashland for many years. His pens featured the Pyle strain, which he brought down to Ashland from his boyhood home in Maryland. The descendants of these birds were the pride of the master and his favored servants. In later years, a friend in Mobile asked for a setting of this famous stock, and a Negro yardman (also from Maryland) was dispatched to secure the eggs. At the time, the Colonel was not aware of the colored man's personal interest in the sporting breed, but his pride was evident later. At the end of the hatching period, the Mobile friend mentioned to the Colonel that not a single bird had hatched. The strange failure was discussed with the servant, who replied with conviction, "Yas suh, I know about it. I shook the hell out of 'em, that's why they won't hatch!"[151]

Domestic responsibilities absorbed most of Mrs. Wilson's hours, but she found time to add a few hundred words each month to the manuscript of her sixth novel. Finally in the spring of 1875 she sent the finished book to Carleton. *Infelice* follows the sentimental-didactic pattern of her earlier successes, but the emotional scenes are far more melodramatic than anything she had written before. This story about the theatre is strongly influenced by the "big curtains" of the contemporary stage: those tearful, intense scenes which were devised to wring the last tear from a willing audience. A suggestion of Mrs. Wilson's tendency to overdo her effects is observed in her choice of the heroine's theatrical name, Mrs. Odille Orphia Orme, which sounds as mournful as the poor actress's agonizing speeches. The big scenes of *Infelice* are strictly in the tradition of melodrama: a famous actress plays her part so well that she leads her bigamous husband and his degenerate father to make indiscreet proposals, neither being aware of her identity. Finally, each libertine is exposed when the tragedienne re-enacts on the Parisian stage the episodes from her earlier life in which the two men had caused her sorrow.

Perhaps Mrs. Wilson's most sympathetic treatment of childhood is to be found in this book. She once admitted to Maddie Wilson Gaillard that she had used her as a model for little Regina, the actress's daughter, whose longing for her absent mother creates many a tearful scene.

Infelice is the least known of her novels, but its sale was respectable in the seventies and eighties. A dramatic version of the novel was composed and copyrighted by Wisner Gillette Scott in December, 1878, but no records of performances have been found. An English photoplay of *Infelice* was released about twenty-five years ago.[152] Two publishers were still listing the book in 1912, and one in 1928. It is apparently out of print at the present time.

In February, 1878, the quiet routine of Ashland was disturbed by the critical illness of Augusta's mother, who was still residing at Georgia Cottage. Since the novelist's childhood, the strongest influence in her life had been Sarah Howard Evans, the calm and thoughtful mother who occupied the unusual position in her daughter's life of tutor and confidential friend. Years of successful authorship and marriage into a wealthy circle appeared to strengthen the bond between them. Though Augusta was seldom demonstrative, she made an exception of her love for Mrs. Evans, often citing her deep appreciation for her mother's guidance and affection. Augusta reinforced her flattering tributes with many acts of kindness. Only serious illness at Ashland or absence from Mobile ever prevented her from visiting Georgia Cottage each day. The death of Mrs. Evans on February 5, 1878, was the greatest sorrow of Augusta's life up to this time.

With the exception of this deep personal grief, Mrs. Wilson's life reached a quiet plateau in the late seventies which lasted until 1891. Her daily routine was rich in many specialized interests, as we have seen, but her personal friendships were valued as highly as her domestic, literary and intellectual pursuits. For twenty years, her closest friend had been Mrs. Rachel Lyons Heustis, and they continued to see each other very often for the next thirty years. After Frank Crawford became Mrs. Cornelius Vanderbilt, they visited each other every year or so; as a token of her love, Mrs. Vanderbilt requested on her deathbed that one of her valuable possessions be sent to Augusta, and the relatives later forwarded a costly diamond bracelet. Another good friend was a cloistered nun, Mother Mary Stanislaus of the Convent of the Visitation, whom Augusta visited as often as possible, but "Stanislaus" (as she often referred to the Mother Superior) was able to return the calls only at the rarest intervals. Twice when her order sent her out on important missions (one of which was to establish a convent in Mexico), she paid brief visits to Ashland. The youthful opposition of Augusta to the doctrines of the Catholic Church, which had colored every chapter of *Inez* back in the fifties, was no longer expressed. She remained biased on many subjects (one of the special and prized qualities of all Victorians), but her mature tolerance in matters of religion is evidenced by her choice of close friends: Mrs. Heustis, who was reared as an orthodox Jew; Mother Stanislaus, a leader in the Catholic world; and Bishop Richard H. Wilmer, highly respected head of the Mobile diocese of the Episcopal Church. "Stanislaus is a superwoman," Augusta once remarked. Bishop Wilmer's portrait was the only one outside her immediate family which she displayed in her household.

The respect which the Bishop had for Mrs. Wilson's intellectual powers was matched by her high regard for his mind and abilities. Throughout their long friendship both obtained much pleasure from their playful intellectual repartee, especially on the subject of the Bishop's winning Mrs. Wilson to his faith. Once when she consulted him on the propriety of her sponsoring a child in a notable christening in his church, the Bishop assured her that she might be a Godmother in an Episcopal service, and he added jokingly, referring to his desire to confirm her in his faith, "And I will scratch *your* head yet!" But she remained a loyal Methodist.

In the late nineties Bishop Wilmer agreed to assist Mrs. Wilson in one of her favorite projects, the establishment of a nonsectarian infirmary and nursing school. The novelist called a meeting of a group of interested citizens in January, 1896, and she persuaded Bishop Wilmer to preside. When it came time to name the hospital, interested friends proposed the names of Mrs. Wilson and the Bishop, but both declined on the grounds that the infirmary should be non-sectarian, and each was intimately associated with particular sects. Mrs.

Wilson made a memorial gift to the Mobile Infirmary in honor of her husband, and one section of the structure was named the "L. M. Wilson Ward."

The interval of twelve years between her sixth and seventh novels was due mainly to her weakened health, but there was no cessation of charitable interests and domestic responsibilities, especially gardening, nor of flights to escape the dreaded attacks of hay fever. Her suffering was so great in the spring and fall that she was forced to abandon reading and writing for months at a time, but year by year she added chapters to her latest romance, one which she came to like more than any previous work.

At the Mercy of Tiberius was ready for the publisher in the summer of 1887. The exceptional amount of realism in this book, as compared with other examples of domestic sentimentalism, makes us wonder if Mrs. Wilson had at last succumbed to the dominant critical standards of the day: that fiction should present life as it is, regardless of the author's moral or sentimental objections to many plain facts of life in America. This book is in no sense a muck-raker or a representative example of local color, but many critical readers must have been pleased to see that exotic, non-American plants, beasts, and architectural designs are nearly eliminated in favor of bird dogs, scuppernong arbors and recognizable colonial mansions. Also, *Tiberius* contains many natural conversations, some even in Negro dialect, and a host of superstitions, folk customs, and probable daily trivialities, all of which are more entertaining to a modern reader than the strained scholarship, stiff dialogue, and undeveloped pathetic episodes which dominated her earlier books. In handling customs and speech, she had the advice of a talented writer of short stories in Negro dialect, Mrs. E. W. Bellamy, one of her close friends. *Tiberius* is the most Southern of her novels, and perhaps this is why she often said that it was her favorite.

The author's new interest in realism did not cause her to neglect sentiment; as a whole, *Tiberius* probably stimulates more pathos than it does social consciousness or aesthetic surprise. Once more Mrs. Wilson's heroine is more complex than the traditional meek, "Amelia" type of woman whom other sentimentalists (except Charlotte Bronte) had been content to use, but the misfortunes which plague Beryl are developed more with the view of squeezing tears from the reader than as natural consequences of the fictional problem which the author has chosen. Like Jane Eyre (as well as Beulah and Edna Earl) Beryl is endowed with intellectual stamina and exceptional talents, along with her moral fortitude, kindliness, forbearance and Christian hope. The climactic scenes are heavily charged with melodrama, as were the big curtains of *Infelice,* but in preparation for them, we are introduced to many things which are treated without sentiment or moralizing: a well constructed detective story, an exciting trial for murder, pleasant glimpses of mansion life on a Southern plantation, humor in Negro dialect and manners, some plausible local color, and very few examples of fine writing. There are intimations, however, that a tear-jerker will emerge from the realistic mystery story, for the heroine cannot establish her alibi in the murder trial without implicating her brother, and she had faithfully promised her dying mother that she would always protect this wayward boy.

After Beryl allows herself to be convicted on circumstantial evidence of a crime she did not commit, the pathos of her martyrdom in prison is revealed in Mrs. Wilson's best agonizing manner. In the second half of the book, we see the brave, talented girl nursing the hardened criminals, helping them to pray for their souls, caring for an illegitimate daughter of a prisoner, organizing Bible classes, and in all ways demonstrating the faith and charity of a noble woman. Finally, the remorseful prosecutor, who had fallen in love with Beryl during the trial (his interesting problem of passion versus legal integrity is not fully explored), discovers the one person who can absolve Beryl: her brother. The author has a surprise for us here. The brother's innocence is dramatically revealed in the discovery that a *lightning photograph* had been imprinted miraculously upon a pane of glass, and this picture reveals that a bolt of lightning had caused the death, and not Beryl or her brother. Thus, a story which might have been a clever murder mystery, if Mrs. Wilson had been that kind of writer, or an exposure of judicial evils (circumstantial evidence and bad penal practices) if the author had leaned toward social consciousness, is fashioned into a moral melodrama. Its audience is moved by personal sorrows, not by the blunders of society.

Mrs. Wilson was very proud of her use of the pseudo-scientific trick of electrical photography. She wrote a friend that she could afford to laugh at reviewers who ridiculed the incident of lightning: "... Before the novel was written I had carefully investigated electrical phenomena, and had collected accounts of *four or five well authenticated instances of faces photographed on window panes by flashes of lightning.*"[153] It may be that the popularity of *Tiberius* is responsible for the development of a folk myth in Alabama concerning numerous instances of this strange phenomenon, but whatever the origin of the folklore may be, the number of recorded examples of lightning photography and the mystical acceptance of its possibility are as striking as the yarn about the stars which fell on Alabama.

Perhaps the most interesting and best authenticated case of lightning photography is that associated with Carrollton, Alabama, where an ex-slave by the name of Henry Wells was imprisoned in the year 1876 after he admitted setting fire to the Pickens County courthouse. There are several versions of this story, but the most prevalent one is that Wells was hidden in an upper story of the courthouse after reports reached the sheriff that he might be lynched. One stormy night as the frightened Negro peered down into the public square, he thought he saw a mob gathering, and at the height of his terror a bolt of lightning ripped the sky and photographed his fear-crazed face upon the window pane, as the story is related. This image in the glass remained a public curiosity in Carrollton for many years.[154]

Another occurrence of lightning photography took place in the house of Mrs. Wilson's uncle, Dr. Norborne

B. Powell of Chunnenuggee Ridge, Alabama, in about the year 1873. Relatives testify that the image of Dr. Powell's wife was photographed on a pane of glass during a severe electrical storm. Mrs. Powell's distinctive cap and her large cameo pin were recognizable in the picture, we are told. In the year 1911 the glass was purchased by a grandson of the lady in the miraculous image, Dr. Edward H. Cary, who in recent years has served as president of the American Medical Association and president of Southwestern Medical College. Dr. Cary kept the glass for several years and then repented its removal from Alabama. In about the year 1920 he sent the glass to the Alabama Department of Archives, but shortly thereafter it was shattered beyond repair.[155]

There are other notable cases of lightning photography, but the state of Alabama seems to have produced more than its share of them. One cannot help wondering if Mrs. Wilson's treatment of this strange incident, together with the author's record of moral earnestness in her works and life, have not given greater credence to the myth than otherwise might have occurred.

The scientists of the Corning Glass Works, who have done the most extensive experimentation in the negative properties of glass in photography, have written this author that no known common glass manufactured in the nineteenth century could have received a photographic image. These technicians have recently perfected a glass on which pictures may be photographed, but such a glass is radically different from all previous window panes.[156] Numerous physicists have shaken their heads at the suggestion that the incidents at Chunnenuggee Ridge, Carrollton, and in *Tiberius* can be explained by the laws of physics—that is, if we can mean that the lightning served as the camera and the glass as the negative—but all of them hasten to add that severe heat might etch an image in glass, through cracking or through its effects upon the irridescence native to the glass. Dr. Edward H. Cary is willing to admit that "some unknown ray occurring in the thunderstorm" is responsible for the image of his grandmother, but he does not argue that lightning can take the place of a camera.[157] The Corning scientists point out that under the circumstances of the recorded cases, the object being photographed (a person) must be posed between the camera (lightning) and the negative (glass); thus the cases at Carrollton and in *Tiberius* are not physically possible because the two subjects are *inside* the buildings, with the glass between them and the supposed "camera."

But perhaps the laws of physics are out of place in an atmosphere of folklore. Many readers, particularly Alabamians, are convinced that the heroine of *Tiberius* and her brother are innocent of the murder because the shrewd authoress used an experience familiar to many people. That is the way myths are born.

Tiberius was dramatized by an Australian named William J. Reside, who copyrighted his version on December 22, 1904. He sent a copy of his play to Mrs. Wilson and requested that she give her permission for its presentation in London, but she returned the manuscript with demands for certain alterations.[158] No record has been found of a production by Mr. Reside, although someone's adaptation of *Tiberius* had a successful run of four weeks in Chicago in the year 1911.[159] Several people recall a good movie based on the novel and entitled "God's Witness," released about the year 1920.[160]

Perhaps the most flattering praise given to one of Mrs. Wilson's late books was the defence of *Tiberius* by Professor W. S. Wyman, scholar of Latin and Greek and three times acting president of the University of Alabama, against the attacks printed in the Montgomery *Advertiser*.[161] He argues that Mrs. Wilson again "laughs at the critics of the high cockalorum school, who have failed now for the seventh time to set aside the judgment of the literary public touching the merit of her work." The professor summarizes the objections of the Montgomery critic: "First, that Mrs. Wilson's novels make us cry. Second, that the author uses too many big words."

Few sentimental Victorians would disagree with the first point in Professor Wyman's rebuttal: he argues that "any work that stirs the nobler passions in a cultured soul is not only a good book and a successful book, but is a work of high art and is so far forth a product of genius." As for the lack of realism in her books, he states that a novelist's or poet's "beautiful ideal" is something that "nobody has ever seen or heard of in nature or real life," because "the highest truth of art, which it is the work of genius to elaborate, is altogether and purely ideal." Photographic realism is only one criterion of criticism and not a very reliable one, the classical scholar reasons. Only the "literary ennuyé" sighs for "the realism of Henry James, Jr., of Alphonse Daudet, or of Zola." Mrs. Wilson's novels satisfy the great majority of readers because these books are "genuine romances of a very high order, such as the educated public likes; and, as the enlightened public does not care a fig for the naturalistic element in fiction, it buys Mrs. Wilson's books and reads them."

As for the charge that her books have too many unfamiliar words and quotations—the basis for most of the attacks upon her novels—Professor Wyman answers tartly, "Nothing is droller than the general reluctance of the critical intellect to confess its own inferiority." He assumes that her erudition and allusiveness are merits too obvious for direct comment.

A week later Professor Wyman resumes the debate, again in the most conspicuous column on page one of the Tuscaloosa *Gazette*. He is sorry to see that the *Advertiser* has violated the "impersonality" which editorialists require by identifying him, but he is more concerned about the rival newspaper's charge that Mrs. Wilson's books are read and admired mainly by "children and negroes and other uneducated folk." He believes that they are read by "the most intelligent, and refined, and highly-educated grown people of these United States and of England," not only because these readers find them "excellent . . . by all the tests that good literary work ought to be judged," but because her books "make people better . . . are uplifting . . . have a certain educational value, after the order of Scott's novels." The "learning" in them should be commended by critics, especially since the public likes it. The Professor states that he inquired about the sale of *Tiberius* at the Tuscaloosa bookstore and found that thirty copies of this book had been sold to one of the other "cloth-bound novels." He was informed that for many years Mrs. Wilson's novels have been "standard and staple goods on the shelves of the booksellers."

The novelist wrote a long letter of thanks for this answer to "the persistent phillippics of the Montgomery *Advertiser*."[162] She is proud to have the "championship of Tuscaloosa—the acknowledged seat of culture and classical learning in Alabama," but throughout her career she never had doubted that "the vast body of American readers are sufficiently enlightened and just to discriminate between coarse abuse, vulgar sneers and flippant jeering" of journalistic critics and true criticism: "that dispassionate, impersonal, faithful analysis of literary work." She cites Andrew Lang's essay, "Realism and Romance" (which favors romance as opposed to realism on grounds similar to those advanced by Professor Wyman), as an excellent example of "genial tolerance" and "generous catholicity" in criticism. Thomas Carlyle is also quoted at length in defence of fashionable novels which instill "some good," and thus cannot be charged with "absolute vacuity." The public seems to agree with the great Victorian who says to "Novelwrights: therefore, write on Brother, even as thou canst, even as it has been given thee."

A flippant reviewer for the New York *Tribune* chooses to laugh at the style of *Tiberius* by pretending to defend its "talk that never was on land or sea," but this critic disparages, in apparent innocence, the very quality of her style which attracted thousands of readers: "The world in which [Mrs. Wilson] moves is one from which the rest of us are excluded; the atmosphere of which perhaps we could not breathe; the denisons of which we fail to recognize as being akin to our common humanity. But is it not cause for humble thankfulness that we have among us an author capable, even at twelve-year intervals, of lifting us far above the carping care of this sordid sphere, and bathing our spirits, so to speak, in the refined and refining medium through which her own floats so buoyantly."[163] He believes it is this "persistent and courageous gilding of our petty lives which is the distinguishing characteristic of Mrs. Wilson . . . the luxuriant optimism, the lexicographic opulence of her expressions." He cites this quality as the reason why discerning readers will avoid *Tiberius*: "It is true that a little of this kind of fiction goes a long way, and perhaps once in twelve years is quite as often as the public ought to be placed 'at the mercy of Tiberius.' " But thousands of readers believed that the strange luxuries of style and setting in those books are in keeping with the tone of high seriousness which Mrs. Wilson maintains. Likewise, the vast stores of erudition and the elevation of language were considered a fitting medium for the mighty struggles of conscience in which the gifted characters reveal their superiority to the common run of humanity.

CHAPTER XV

Last Days

1887-1909

IN THE YEAR 1891 Mr. Wilson was eighty-three years old and Augusta was fifty-six. Much success had come to each of them in their separate fields of interest, but both considered their marriage and their life at Ashland to be the primary interest of their lives. Perhaps their store of tolerance and understanding was often tested by unusual hobbies and talents, but nothing interfered with their mutual joy in the comfortable social life of Ashland. Prosperity, public acclaim, a host of admiring friends, but especially their own common sense, had contributed to a married life which each considered ideal.

In spite of Mr. Wilson's advancing years, Augusta apparently did not want to think about the certainty of his passing, for when his final illness came and his death on October 7, 1891, she was stunned by the finality of the change. She had made no definite plans. Of only one decision was she convinced: she could never live at Ashland again. Everything there reminded her of Mr. Wilson—the moss-laden liveoaks which he had planted as acorns nearly sixty years before; the splendid lawns of bermuda, the camellias, hot-houses, and crowing gamecocks, every sight and sound of the old place was associated with the vigorous, dignified, sporting gentleman who had meant more to her than a lifetime of literary successes. She could not bear to live with them in his absence.

In obedience to Augusta's wishes, Mr. Wilson had made out his will principally in favor of his children and grandchildren by the first marriage, leaving the property at Ashland to Mrs. Fannie Wilson Jordan, Miss Maddie Wilson (who married S. Palmer Gaillard in 1893), and Mr. Albert Wilson. By agreement with all the heirs, Augusta purchased Albert's share of this property. Colonel Wilson had wisely invested the enormous earnings of the novelist since 1867, and she did not need the bulk of his large estate. By the standards of that day, Mrs. Wilson was independently wealthy.

About a year after her husband's death, Augusta obtained the consent of the co-owners of Ashland to close the estate. She was uncertain about permanent plans for herself, but she wished to live near her sister, Mrs. Virginia Bragg, whose house was then crowded with four growing children and her brother, Howard Evans. Mrs. Wilson spent a few months with a close friend, Mrs. Anna M. Fosdick, and then she persuaded Mrs. Bragg to let her use the "back parlor" of the Bragg house temporarily, which she did until she found a house for sale nearby, at 255 State Street. She lived there until 1894, when Mrs. Bragg decided to build in a more westerly residential section, and then Mrs. Wilson purchased the massive house at 930 Government

Street, within walking distance of the Braggs and the Wilson relatives; also, the home of her brother Randolph was not too far away. The remaining fifteen years of her life were spent in this enormous Victorian townhouse.

The Ashland property was not sold until 1907, when Mr. George Fearn, Jr., purchased it and hired a famous architect to restore the mansion. The grounds of the estate were sub-divided into large lots, and soon many comfortable houses were built in the new development. In 1920 the Wilson mansion was sold to the Armbrecht family, who graciously allowed visitors to inspect it until a fire destroyed the entire structure in the year 1926. The residential section is still known as Ashland Place.

Mrs. Wilson's declining years were not spent entirely with her memories, but like most Victorian widows—and possibly at the suggestion of the queenly "widow of Windsor"—she cherished her loss with an almost morbid intensity. We cannot grasp fully the Victorian style of things unless we take account of their responses to the tragic crises of life, especially those associated with illness, death and mourning. Most popular novels and dramas of the day echo their concern with the deathbed scene. Many of their popular songs and illustrations express tearful sorrow over parting. Outward signs of respect for the dead were not merely fashionable; they were taken for granted in every walk of life. Widow's weeds were the commonest of these observances, but there were others which have almost disappeared by now. All social engagements were taboo for at least a year in each house of mourning, and longer in many cases. References to widows were cast in such tones as to suggest a holiness about the circumstance. For years after Mr. Wilson's death, the novelist used personal correspondence paper with a heavy border of black. Her poor health was partly responsible, but most of Mrs. Wilson's letters during her widowhood refer to her present state as if it were a shadow of the Ashland days, as if life were hardly worth living without the Colonel.

We would not wish to infer that the Victorian widows made an ostentatious display of mourning because it was expected of them. The degree of their sincerity is irrelevant—the point is that they, like all contemporaries who shared their code of living, insisted upon committing themselves openly to certain fixed standards, and deep sorrow over death was considered one of their convictions worth demonstrating publicly. Thousands of people today would hasten to commend the motive behind this old-fashioned way of thinking—the urge to put oneself on record with respect to the worthy standards of life. Sophisticates who smilingly designate this motive as mere exhibitionism have lost touch with the vibrant morality which once stimulated large areas of public opinion.

One solace during these saddened years was Augusta's companionship with Howard Evans. For over twenty years Howard's Sunday afternoon visits to Ashland had been as regular as his Sunday morning attendance at church, and when Augusta left Ashland she invited him to make his home with her. Many people commented on her tender, solicitous regard for this gentle brother, who returned her affection with a love that approached idolatry. Howard's quiet disposition and courteous manner harmonized perfectly with Augusta's temperament, and the two sensitive people fell into an easy routine of life in which each was strongly dependent upon the other.

On Friday the frail couple made their weekly pilgrimage to the cemetery, a day when there would be few visitors there. Augusta's arms were filled with large bouquets of flowers and ferns from her conservatory, and Howard carried the pitcher for watering. This weekly rite was another testimonial in their code of living. The past they loved was renewed as they decorated the graves of father and mother, of the Colonel and his son, of children and neighbors they had been happy with, as well as the tall memorial which Augusta had caused to be erected over the graves of the Confederate dead.

Sometimes one of the devoted servants—Melinda the cook, or Uncle Jerry the coachman, or his wife Fannie the housemaid—accompanied them and paid respects to the departed members of a family to which these colored people were attached for life. The mutual affection and respect which Mrs. Wilson and her servants had for each other is another symbol of a Southern way of life that is changing. At the large Government Street house where employer and employees lived under the same roof, the colored servants were probably the major links between the present and the happier Ashland days. Melinda, Jerry and Fannie gave continuity to the familiar household customs: the efficient regulation of all chores by the clock, assistance in the care of treasured plants, and the tedious preparation of beaten biscuits each morning before dawn. Fannie gave such zealous protection to her mistress's privacy that one visitor called her the "dragon at the gate." The old personal tie between the colored servant family and its white employers, a natural holdover of slavery, is not entirely gone in our time, but few non-Southerners can understand the privileges and affection which accompany it. Another instance is seen in the earlier cook at Ashland, a blue-eyed ex-slave whom everyone called Aunt Ann, who was a regular worshipper in the white Government Street Presbyterian Church, from which she was buried with full rites by the white minister, Dr. J. R. Burgett. Each Sunday she appeared in her black silk dress and occupied her own pew in the gallery.

It is recalled that Howard Evans ventured into Mobile's social life on one occasion each year: to pay his respects to old friends on New Year's Day. Many established families announced their open houses in the newspapers, listing the belles and matrons who would "receive" at each house, for it was the custom for the ladies to entertain the gentlemen on this occasion. Dressed in the fashionable evening gowns which they had worn at the balls the night before, the ladies drew the blinds at two in the afternoon, turned on the lights and awaited their callers, who likewise wore full evening dress and arrived in rented carriages, in groups of four or five. Augusta was often too feeble to entertain on New Year's Day, but she had a habit of enticing several debutantes to slip by her house during the day to let her hear the latest gossip. At other times, however, when the weather was warm enough, she walked to the houses of friends or relatives, or invited them to sit on her high veranda above the busy street. One wit said of her, "Mrs. Wilson is like God—she sits on high and knows everybody."

Her lifelong habit of extensive reading was continued as long as her sight permitted, but she was gradually growing blind in one eye as a result of neuritis. Her brother or Lily Bragg often read to her, from a favorite quarterly or the *National Geographic Magazine*. She did not have a high regard for contemporary fiction, except the novels of Mrs. Humphrey Ward, whose *Helbeck of Bannisdale* prompted her to remark to Lily, "As you children say, 'she beats us all.'" At this time the subject of Spiritualism interested her deeply, but she never admitted a positive belief in it. She once said to Lily Bragg, "If there is any means of communicating with the living after death, you will hear from me."

Her old-fashioned tastes never became accustomed to the rapid progress of the twentieth century. Long after the incandescent bulb was perfected and widely used, her house remained lighted with gas. Since childhood she had been afraid of lightning, and this fear was carried over to the newer electrical devices, especially the telephone, which was not allowed in her house until Mrs. Virginia Bragg came to live with her, even though conversations with friends had always been a source of much pleasure to her. The modern practice of writing checks for all bills did not please her either, and until her death she always paid debts (even doctors' bills) from the large store of cash which she carried in the deep pockets of her woolen wrap. Every outer garment which she owned was provided with these cavernous pockets for the storage of letters, keys and cash.

Her appearance and conversation in the year 1898 are described by LeDeon: "Most people [picture] her as a grave, sombre woman, somewhat austere and haloed, with a nimbus of interwoven science and frigidity. They imagine her a petticoated pundit, saturated with booklore and liable to exude hard words, quotations and intricate problems at slightest touch. In actual truth . . . Mobile holds no simpler, gentler and more domestic woman than she; none more devoted to her home and its inmates, and her favorite dumb pets, both animal and floral. A slim, supple figure of medium height is crowned by the masses of soft brown hair that frame the quiet, thoughtful face." Though her hair is partly white at this time and her lips show traces of sadness, he writes, "the cordial gleam of the still bright eyes and the rare, genuine warmth of her smile quickly veil this [sadness] from friends . . . She is constantly on the go, moving about her house and garden or walking long distances to homes of step-children, step-grandchildren, sisters and nieces at distant points, in all of whom she takes the keenest and most motherly interest."[164]

During the nineties Mrs. Wilson's seven novels were

mentioned by the critics in condescending or nostalgic tones, but DeLeon testifies that their sale continued to produce a handsome income of about $7,000 annually until she sold all rights to her publishers.[165] He writes enviously, "I have been somewhat a traveler myself in the less wild jungles of the Occidental book trade; and often in moments of enforced waiting for the train I have asked proprietors, 'What is your best selling book?' Almost invariably, if slightly varied in locality, the reply received at Denver would be repeated: 'Well, books as is books—bound books, in the long run there's none that equals 'Gusta Evans's.' "[166]

At the turn of the century, Augusta's friends and relatives assumed that her literary career was at an end. Her saddened disposition, her greater interest in the past than in the present or future, and particularly her weak heart and poor eyesight were unfitting accompaniments to authorship, they thought. But they did not reckon with an active mind which had not been weakened by her bodily complaints. Once more, as in her adolescence when she was composing *Inez,* Augusta coyly approached the task of creating a new romance, telling only her brother and the servants about her work. Friends and relatives were amazed when *A Speckled Bird* appeared on the counters in the late summer of 1902.

The fifteen intervening years between *Tiberius* and this latest book had not dimmed Mrs. Wilson's popularity, for her name was sufficient to create a surprising demand for this old-fashioned romance. DeLeon states that "the first edition of 35,000 copies was sold in advance of publication."[167] Within four weeks the novel had reached its third edition.[168] A critic in Brooklyn probably had the best explanation for the appeal of a book so unlike others of the time: "Reading it is like an echo of a day long since dead . . . There are the same social standards . . . and bookish lore flowing smoothly through the stilted dialogue, the absolute neatness of retort and repartee withal, the air of stiff repose . . . And it is so unworldly of the world of to-day that the reader, wearied with the strident and strenuous fiction of this year of our Lord, will be likely to turn to this tale and enjoy its antique spirit with a feeling of absolute restfulness." This reviewer believes that the name of Augusta Evans Wilson will sell many copies, but "old-time novel readers, those whose memories run back thirty years or more, will be likely to welcome this book as a remembrancer, to thank this cultivated Southern gentlewoman for the story and to feel grateful that whatever the world and they have done, she has not changed."[169] Here was proof, the critic seemed to think, that the old times were good; here was flattering assurance that one's youth might be re-captured in spirit.

Loyal followers of domestic sentimentalism (the largest reading public America has ever known) expected to shed copious tears over familiar pathetic situations in *A Speckled Bird,* but Mrs. Wilson surprised many of them by inserting a modern theme into the most agonizing passages of her minor plot. After a rich husband deserts one of the noble characters, Mrs. Nona Dane, this vigorous woman develops a phobia against capitalism and begins to mingle with socialists and anarchists. Soon she loses her respect for religion, and as her Godlessness increases she becomes a "de-sexed feminist" who ignores "the barriers God set between men and women." Finally, she accepts the leadership of a band of labor agitators. We are led to believe that this is about as low as a woman can sink. Only death can now resolve this problem satisfactorily.

The author is not concerned with the economic causes of labor disputes but rather with the inward conflict in Mrs. Dane. The thesis is that women who permit themselves to be "corrupted" by association with the impersonal, materialistic forces of commerce can expect to lose their identity as women, because the hardened practices of business will destroy the delicate, superior moral fibres of feminine character. The fate of Mrs. Dane is exhibited as an object lesson to women who are tempted to follow the affairs of the world as a substitute for their special duties at the hearthstone. Thus Mrs. Wilson's treatment of the liveliest social question of the day, the "rights of women" in politics and business, is heavily conditioned by conservative sentimental thinking, but she does manage to incorporate enough realistic detail about strikes and unionization to suggest that the liberal movement toward realism—led by Twain, Howells, Kirkland, Crane and Dreiser—was forcing a highly successful sentimental moralist to make concessions to naturalism. We would not infer, however, that she was beginning to accept the premises of economic determinism. Her thinking went deeper into the roots of evil, as she saw it. Her position was that the ills of the world are a result of mankind's failure to follow a Christian code of principles (including woman's allegiance to her established place in life), and that economic inequalities cannot be remedied until this primary moral vacuum is filled with brotherly love and Christian faith. Reform which concentrates upon economic injustices will leave the basic disease untouched.

Few contemporary critics found fault with Mrs. Wilson's conservatism in morals and politics. The effects of her philosophy upon literature were certainly deplored by liberal thinkers, but they made the mistake of ignoring such conservatism and thus weakened their own cause by failure to understand the opposition fully, a mistake which intellectual liberals commit in most generations. Those who did read Mrs. Wilson's books and recorded their impressions, also failed to recognize the broad implications of the basic conflict in which she was an important crusader, a conflict which posed reason against faith in philosophy, set naturalism against idealistic romance in fiction, and matched socialized planning against laissez-faire economics. Early battle lines in this conflict were undoubtedly more obscure to participants than they appear to us, but these paired oppositions suggest broadly the loyalties of a liberal or a conservative, though an individual's stand might vary in different fields of thought. Mrs. Wilson's conservatism, however, was uniformly consistent in all important matters, and herein lies the significance of her books: their abundance of testimonials in favor of a conservative way of life that was harshly challenged by newer freedoms in science, in social relations, and in literature.

Adverse criticism of *A Speckled Bird* featured the old complaint about her stilted dialogue and erudite terminology. *Bookman* published a review that so angered Mrs. Wilson by its aloof sarcasm on her language that she composed a stinging reply and sent it to the editor, "darkly hinting" (so he says) that the magazine "would not dare to print it." But the editor shrewdly recognized the commercial value of a quarrel between a popular author and a member of his staff, and made arrangements to publish not only the novelist's "Fable" against critics, but a reprint of the objectionable review, the two in adjacent columns.[170]

Mrs. Wilson answers "the stray female cat's" charges that her latest novel is an "incongruous mythological jumble of ancient style and up-to-date affectations" by permitting her "speckled bird" to argue:

> For fifty years hawks and owls have chased my brothers and sisters in vain, and the vultures are tired waiting for them to die. We shall see all you self-appointed appraisers of literature in your quiet grave. We are here to stay just so long as the world wants us. The reading public is patient and good natured, but knows exactly what it likes, and when a tribe of "rough riders" . . . crack the "true literature" whip too often, the dear obstinate people sometimes "buck" suddenly . . . and these self-commissioned prophets of "review" sanctums find dust in their infallible eyes.

She was assuming that the public wanted what it got—and the sales of the book supported this view—but possibly the critic implied that the public would have been equally satisfied with a product of higher quality. This question is always baffling, but the astonishing popularity of such a dull novel left the victory with Mrs. Wilson: a hundred thousand copies of *A Speckled Bird* were sold within a month of its appearance, if Dillingham's claims can be believed, and the publisher was predicting in August that two hundred thousand copies would be sold before the end of the year.[171]

There was also some journalistic acclaim for her latest book, but Mrs. Wilson gave the chief credit for her success to a loyal public which loved her "high, sweet tones," as she described her style. Hundreds of letters came from her readers, and her habit of answering in her own handwriting was continued while she had the strength. Later Howard Evans and Lily Bragg did the writing at her dictation.

Augusta's earlier custom of traveling widely over the continent was almost abandoned after 1891. An occasional visit was made to her sister Sally in Birmingham, who had married J. W. Bush. She went to New York for the last time in the nineties, to see Fannie Wilson (now Mrs. Frank Jordan), but few other trips were made after her husband's death. Fannie was distressed to observe that her step-mother still dressed in the styles of earlier decades. She remembered Mrs. Wilson's excellent taste in clothes during the Ashland days, as well as the care which the novelist had taken in the attire of her prosperous feminine characters. Once while shopping with Mrs. Wilson, Fannie spied a fashionable wrap which she hoped would atone for the loosely fitting mourning clothes, but she realized that great tact must be exercised to bring about the purchase. She held it before the novelist and exclaimed, "Oh Mama, do take this one. It is so widowy." The strategy worked and the wrap was bought, but when Augusta later described the scene with amusement, she insisted that Fannie's coinage of the apt word "widowy" was the sales point—as well as the warm material of the wrap.

At age seventy-two, and just twenty-one months before her death, Mrs. Wilson received one of her most flattering assurances that her public still clamored for old-fashioned romance. For several months she had been dictating a short story to her favorite niece, Miss Lily Bragg, a narrative entitled *Devota* which was intended for magazine publication. None of her previous fictional works had made their first appearance in magazines, and when Dillingham heard about this story of only thirteen thousand words, he pleaded with the author to let him dress it up for book publication, assuring her that the vast audience which had bought her stout volumes was just as eager to purchase a thin one. She agreed, and *Devota* appeared in large type, the text neatly boxed within ample margins which contained an elaborate floral design. The little volume also offered the sentimental reader four selections from the most popular illustrator of the period, Stuart Travis, whose mauve colorings were the kind which sickened Whistler and prompted him to quip so aptly of decadent Victorianism and its art, "Mauve, mauve—pink trying to be purple."

Devota presents little change in the ideal character-types who dominate most novels of domestic romance. The problem in the action is again a moral conflict, just as personal and sentimental as those faced by Beulah,

Edna Earl, Vashti, and other heroines: can a proud, cultured woman accept a marriage proposal from the Governor of her state, in spite of the fact that she had jilted him when he was impoverished and in disgrace? After a long debate between the two cold, intellectual lovers, a common ground of understanding is reached, and they confess their undying love.

In the extensive dialogues of *Devota,* questions of social and philosophical import are continually broached, but the assertions of a small group of wealthy conservatives are allowed to pass unchallenged, and we must assume that their views are also the author's. The demands of the Populist Party are assailed as the "wild craze of greedy, omnivorous, grudging 'Have Nots' " who exhibit "that variety of original sin that claims something for nothing." Portions of the conservative argument have a very modern ring: "Demagogues are persuading the disgruntled of all classes that they are now kicking the vile, corrupt body of corporations, but the inevitable reaction" will come eventually when the public recognizes "the civic equity" of a capitalist's "inalienable right to the fruit of his labor, mental or manual." And the following piece of indignation, expressed by an uncompromising States Rights Democrat, might well have been uttered recently: "The time-honored party name, Democracy, is disgraced by the effort to make it mother a mongrel brood of socialists, whose wild antics and schemes of universal confiscation would cause Thomas Jefferson to gasp." He adds that if the father of the Party could leave his grave, he would "scourge the 'populistic' leaders—now strutting under the standard of his stolen mantle." Other social questions, such as the implications of capital punishment and the best treatment of juvenile delinquents, are debated at some length, but a properly indoctrinated sentimentalist could guess before opening the book that Mrs. Wilson would argue that capital punishment does not harmonize with brotherly love, that all problems of childhood are the responsibility of adults, and that reformatories for children are brutal screens for the mistakes of parents.

In 1913 *Devota* was issued again as a memorial to Mrs. Wilson, and her lifelong friend, Thomas Cooper DeLeon, was commissioned to write a short reminiscence for the edition, but his tribute contains little critical material on her writing and only the most flattering of his recollections of the woman. DeLeon's few remarks on her books have an air of terse condescension—an attitude which would be more acceptable if DeLeon's own creative writing were noticeably different from Mrs. Wilson's or superior to it—but it is likely that his opinions were dictated more by jealousy than by critical insight, for he watched his many volumes go almost unnoticed while Mrs. Wilson's nine romances were bought and discussed everywhere.

Augusta's last days were brightened by many warm friendships. Besides her girlhood chum, Rachel Lyons Heustis, who still kept in close touch with the novelist, there were her physician and good friend, Dr. William M. Mastin and his wife, Margaret; also, Mr. and Mrs. Gaylord B. Clark (Mr. Clark was her lawyer), Mrs. George A. Ketchum and her daughter Mrs. Georgia

Ketchum Gage, Captain and Mrs. A. C. Danner and their daughters; Judge and Mrs. Henry Chamberlain, Mrs. Lee Fearn Irwin, Mrs. John Quill, Mrs. Anna M. Fosdick, and Mrs. Frank J. McCoy.

The relatives who were closest to her at this time, besides Howard Evans, were Mrs. Virginia Bragg, Miss Lily Bragg, Mrs. Maddie Wilson Gaillard, Mr. Randolph Evans (her brother) and his children Clarence and Augusta. Maddie had married S. Palmer Gaillard, a prominent young attorney, and she often brought her five children to the great Victorian house on Government Street to see the noted lady whose swishy taffeta petticoats and tasty beaten biscuits made a deeper impression upon them than the reports of her fame. At the time of Mrs. Gaillard's last illness, in November, 1907, Augusta again demonstrated her dependability and compelling sense of obligation in times of personal crisis. The family doctor relates that he was called at midnight, and when he had harnessed his horse and driven out to the street, he found Mrs. Wilson awaiting him at his gate so that she might accompany him to the Gaillard house in Spring Hill. She was quite infirm at the time, and her house was several blocks from Dr. Fondé's.

Augusta's special solace came from her companionship with Howard Evans, who was helpful in many ways, but particularly as amanuensis after her physical strength became no match for her mental activity. Many losses had been met with fortitude during Augusta's eventful life, but Howard's death on June 5, 1908, was so grievous to her that she never recovered a zest for living, and occasionally she remarked that her days were merely a quiet awaiting of death.

Mrs. Virginia Bragg and three of her children came to live at the large house shortly after Howard's death. Their presence was a comfort to an aging lady who had honored motherhood eloquently in her books but had been denied a child of her own. There had been many young people in her life, though, from the time of her adolescence at Georgia Cottage when seven brothers and sisters had romped through her small study, to the days at Ashland when she had enjoyed the teen-age schemes of Fannie Wilson and the games of little Maddie. For nearly fifty years she had been one of the "Lady Managers" of the Protestant Orphan Asylum, where she had made many lifelong friends among the children. In her last days she again won the confidence of a congenial niece, Miss Lily Bragg, who had taken down the pages of *Devota* in longhand as her famous aunt had dictated, and who constantly delighted Mrs. Wilson with her news of the younger people.

In the spring of 1909 Augusta seemed to know that her end was near. She was heard to speak of her approaching death as if it were a familiar and not unwelcome event. On the day after her seventy-fourth birthday, she suffered a heart attack and died almost immediately. She was buried at Magnolia beside Howard Evans, his stone marked "Brother," hers "Sister." Her funeral was described as the largest ever seen in Mobile, and lengthy obituaries appeared in newspapers throughout the nation. Among the sincerest mourners was Thomas Cooper DeLeon, now completely blind, who sat at his typewriter on the day of her death and tapped out a eulogy which serves as the inscription over her grave:

> Dead! in the fullness of years and fame,
> What has she left?
> High on the roll of fair duty a name,
> Loved; friends devoted, as few women claim:
> A Nation bereft!

She left bequests to her favorite institutions—the St. Francis Street Methodist Church, the Mobile Infirmary, the Protestant Orphanage, and the Y. M. C. A. Each surviving servant was remembered too. The remainder of her estate was divided among many relatives.[172]

Recipe for an Old-fashioned Best Seller

By the time Augusta Jane Evans's first book appeared, American readers were very familiar with the novel of domestic sentimentalism, which depended upon moralizing and pathetic situations for its popular appeal. Nathaniel Hawthorne despondently surveyed the reading tastes of the year 1855 (when *Inez* appeared) and wrote his publisher the following diatribe upon the type of novel which was obviously preferred to his own superior *Scarlet Letter* and *The House of the Seven Gables*:

> America is now wholly given over to a d——d mob of scribbling women, and I should have no chance of success while the public taste is occupied with their trash—and should be ashamed of myself if I did succeed. What is the mystery of these innumerable editions of the "Lamplighter," and other books neither better nor worse?—worse they could not be, and better they need not be, when they sell by the 100,000.[173]

His judgment coincided with the views of the leading critics, but the public continued to ignore their ridicule during the next half century, as it has done up to our time, and went on buying and reading sentimental novels. The "damned mob of scribbling women" who produced these works between 1850 and 1900 repeated patterns of ideas, characterization, pathetic situations, and plot problems with a regularity that appalled the critics but satisfied the publishers and a large constituency.

The popularity of *Pamela, Charlotte Temple, The Coquette, The Lamplighter* and similar early fiction is not the chief reason for this vogue in American Victorian fiction. Before the year 1855 millions of Americans had been trained to believe that *feeling* is an adequate gauge of good conduct and righteous beauty. When Miss Evans and her rivals devoted their best efforts to the moral and pathetic aspects of deathbed scenes, deserted wives, correct manners, and enchanting landscapes, they were imitating earlier fiction or following the philosophical idea of *sensibility* only by accident. Specifically, they were making appeals to a taste which had been molded by the life in their times, at American firesides, in political campaigns, and in the pews of evangelical churches. As one critic puts it, "The yellowed pages [of their novels] reveal the aspirations and hopes, which in its earnest moments, a generation of readers strove to achieve."[174]

Since the exciting days of the Revolution, sentiment had characterized our thinking about liberty and the rights of man, especially under-privileged man; many speakers had defended majority rule on the grounds that most men are motivated by altruism. Sermons and political speeches had given authenticity to extravagance in language on subjects with emotional undercurrents. The theatre had contributed its share in setting the style for language and conduct in pathetic situations, and its audiences, long practiced in the public shedding of tears, would see nothing amiss in the numerous tearful experiences of heroines, or even heroes, in sentimental novels.

An unsophisticated reader who takes a novel in hand and awaits its effect is just as critical as the reviewer, but his mind is likely to be closed to some of the standards which are honored by the professional. Two centuries ago this average reader was indifferent to, or suspicious of, the exciting appeal of *reason.* And the first novelist to seek his favor, Samuel Richardson in *Pamela* (1740), quite shrewdly chose to tell his story in the manner of an evangelical minister who knows the power of sentiment and moralizing upon the majority of minds. A century later, when Augusta Jane Evans began to write, the masses of people could not embrace the impersonal objectivity so dear to the early scientist, because they suspected that the scientific method did not contain a reverence for cherished manners and beliefs. And the authors who wished their patronage (Catherine Maria Sedgwick, Caroline Lee Hentz, Susan Warner, Maria Susanna Cummins, Mrs. E. D. E. N. Southworth, Marion Harland, Mary Jane Holmes, E. P. Roe, and Lew Wallace, to name the most successful of Miss Evans's rivals) not only indicated their respect for older and more personal things, but they sometimes attacked the open-minded spirit in which scientists approach truth. Still a century later, in our own day, the critics' joy in the freedom of the arts or in unashamed naturalism is likely, again, to provoke suspicion within our current average reader, who will turn to Lloyd

Douglas or Dorothy Canfield before he will to Dreiser or Lewis because the former writers, different as they are, have respect for sentiment and traditional concepts. Sentimental ties develop the strongest loyalties, and more than one literary historian has marveled at the continuous enthusiasm of the public for novels of this *genre*. These faithful readers respond to a dignified style and to opulent furnishings because these qualities are suggestive of childhood and grandmother's time. Pathetic tableaux or moralizing passages, which often embarrass sophisticated people, are warmly admired by the average reader, who will defend them because they remind him of older and better times, and because the moods which they evoke are associated with tradition and permanence.

A panoramic view of the people, the messages, and the action which are common to about fifty sentimental best sellers will be sufficient to establish the striking kinship among these books, and at the same time such a view should give many clues concerning the sales value of the most popular form of writing in recent centuries.

All novels of this class have a set of righteous characters—just, kind, handsome, often talented or intellectual, and sometimes tolerant about minor questions—each endowed with sufficient capacity for success in any normal enterprise. These noble people, however, are allowed to skim close to the brink of failure because of their stubborn and sacrificial loyalty to a code of honor or religion, the tenets of which are acceptable to all people in this set and are ignored by their adversaries. From book to book the heroines and heroes, the protective mothers and repentant fashionable ladies, the earnest boys and their ambitious sisters, are repeated so uniformly that in most instances one character might be exchanged for another, in their respective spheres and sexes, with little change in the problems of the different novels.

There is the youthful heroine, frequently an orphan, whose ambitions are thwarted by the privations and slurs incident to poverty, until she becomes a governess or possibly a ward of a patrician family. She is usually the principal figure in the story, because these novels have been written mainly by women for feminine and juvenile audiences. Since good taste in the heroine's circle and among her audience does not permit the author to reveal her physical charms very realistically or to subject her to many temptations, she appears inhumanly perfect. She is deeply religious, very charitable, and easily moved to tears, though the strongest of these women show righteous pride and independence. In earlier novels, the heroine faints in the midst of situations which wound her sensibilities, but this delicate manner is not so common in later works—possibly one good literary influence of the feminist movement.

Youthful companions of the heroine are often more distinctive characters, for they may possess such faults as jealousy, false pride, social ambition, or indifference to religion. Only a few women in these books, however, possess such evil traits as hatred, malice, sensuousness, lying, or physical cruelty. The daughters of fashionable parents are portrayed more fully and realistically than the humble heroines. One amusing type is the gay flirt, whose interests are limited to dancing and beaux, and another is the disillusioned belle, usually a confidante of the noble heroine, who denounces the sins of the idle rich and deplores their shallow religious observances. At least one companion is a foil to the heroine; a girl whose shallowness, worldly standards, and lack of ambition contrast sharply with the leading lady's pursuit of knowledge, her deep faith, and her unostentatious charities.

The mothers are either ideal protectors of their firesides, who administer tenderly to the physical and spiritual needs of their husbands and children, or they are shallow members of the smart set, ever alert to make a good match for their daughters. They may be callous, frivolous and haughty, but they are never aggressively sinful. The evil most frequently charged against the mature women is their encouragement of marriage for gold rather than for true love.

The hero may have a few faults, because it is assumed that man's vigor and his contact with a rough world make self-control and piety difficult of attainment. Also, each mature male must be presented as the object of some good woman's pious influence, for the noble women of these books are universally endowed with a superior intuition, a moral monitor which must guide their families into heaven. The hero is frequently more mature than the heroine, and often does not marry until he is past thirty. He may not be a church member, but he respects religion in name, and after marriage he graciously assents to his wife's campaign to place him on the side of the angels. He demands that his associates show the proper respect for women, whether the delicate creatures are present or absent. He may be a man of property or member of a profession, but he cherishes other intellectual or artistic interests, and his talents must exceed those of the heroine, for every happy wife "looks up to" her husband. Early disappointment in love or in friendship may have turned him into a cynic or misanthrope, but hope and geniality are reawakened by his love for a pure and beautiful girl.

When the sentimental novelists dropped the seduction theme, probably under the influence of Victorian propriety, the fashionable seducer became a wife-deserter, but his guilt is certainly no less severe, for now his sins are against the heart, the home, and his holy vows. Sometimes he is merely a weak boy from fashionable society, whose parents aid him in escaping from an unsuitable match. In this case, he may attempt to right the wrong he has done, and out of his suffering must emerge latent qualities of nobility and ambition. If he is a confirmed and mature scoundrel, without respect for God or feminine virtue, he must meet an ignominious death or be banished from society, usually after exposure by the hero.

An elderly patriarch, who believes in God's justice and man's altruism, frequently appears, either as minister, father, guardian or tutor. His maxims in defence of the home, religion, and social behavior, and his inspiring Christian deathbed scene, influence the young characters and produce beneficent tears.

The thoughts of the good or regenerate characters are usually indistinguishable from the views which the author super-imposes upon the story. Characterization, narration, exposition conspire to teach the standards of conduct and belief which are identified with American Victorianism. A careful reading of these stories will produce object lessons in a variety of situations—the proper treatment of aged parents by sons and daughters, the correct behavior of a young lady in a strange city, the benefits of good business and professional ethics, or the conduct of an actress who would avoid scandal—in fact, there is such an abundance of similar exhibits in the usefulness of decorous conduct and good morals that the social historian may consider these novels as textbooks in America's moral and social education.

Mrs. Wilson is unique among her rivals in that she incorporates philosophical and aesthetic discussions among her emotional materials. These serious problems were presented with the view of widening her audience, and she succeeded because millions of unsophisticated Americans were pathetically culture-conscious during the growing years of our nation. The multiple effect of her books—of sentiment wrapped in broad culture and piety—appealed to many tastes. Such cultural erudition as the hundreds of quotations and references, the critical passages on great painting and music, the learned discussions of ancient history and modern politics might be too allusive and incomplete for the average reader's mental improvement, but this learning did give a tone of high-seriousness to a type of literature which was noted mainly for its emotional, not intellectual, values. If the masses of Americans have always assumed that mere association with the arts, particularly with those which are difficult of comprehension, is culturally beneficial, Mrs. Wilson's erudition must have contributed greatly to her vogue.

In the two centuries of popularity which this species of novel has enjoyed, there is little or no evidence that the masses of readers have found serious fault with the moral tone, the perfect heroines, and the educational expositions of these books, as did numerous professional critics. One answer may be that the books contain enough exciting action and moving pathos to satisfy all tastes for which they are intended. Each book has a love story, in which the "dictates of the heart" are frustrated for a time by such problems as difference in social status, opposition of mercenary parents, lack of religious faith, previous disillusionment in love, or competition from artistic or intellectual interests. Scheming villains and malicious flirts are seldom used to separate the lovers. The most common obstacle in the path of true love is the proposed marriage for money and social position.

Nearly every problem which the major characters face demands that they take a firm moral position, and most of these serious people are willing to wreck their health and lose their happiness in order to find solutions which will satisfy their consciences. They master the arts and philosophies to gain an understanding of the mysteries of beauty and truth, and these pursuits invariably bring them into the company of other ambitious, moral and sentimental people whom they admire and eventually love.

At times the narration of the love story is interrupted by a succession of pathetic situations—tender deathbed scenes of true Christians, awe-inspiring deaths of sinners or infidels, the suffering of lonely orphans—which are developed more fully than is necessary, insofar as they contribute to characterization and action. A blind girl or an impoverished widow may be introduced for no other purpose than to elicit the charity of the heroine and the tears of the reader. Numerous drunkards appear, receive the author's or heroine's lecture on temperance, and then disappear forever.

One very successful technique of sentimental fiction is the use of pathetic or artistic tableaux, which are like scenic purple patches in these novels. The tableaux are ornamental adjuncts to the action, and they could be omitted without serious injury to the novel's structure. Each is like a group statue or painting, the details being carefully selected to enforce a grand or pathetic emotion.

A good example is the scene of little Stanley's escape from the orphan's home in *Vashti.* His sister, Salome, is walking near her old home, a decaying mill, and hears a child crying in the weeds. She discovers that it is her brother, who has escaped from the orphanage because they beat him; he came "home" to the old mill, but the strange man who now lives there threatened to shoot him if he did not go away. He is hungry and begs his sister to take him to her guardian's house. "Everybody else can get a home and why can't we?" he pleads in behalf of himself and another sister; and Salome answers, "Because your father was a drunkard and left his children to the charity of the poor-house." The setting, with the old mill in the background, and the saddened girl holding her little brother on her lap, gives the impression of a tableau, innocently posed.[175]

Many of these brief pathetic scenes have deep religious feeling, particularly the dutiful pilgrimages to "God's Acre," where rests a friend or relative. Sometimes the reader looks upon an isolated tableau of a soul in torture. We see St. Elmo after an interview with the saintly heroine:

> He set his teeth hard, and his fingers clinched as if longing to crush something; and then came a great revulsion, a fierce spasm of remorse, and his features writhed.
>
> "Sinful? Ay! Cruel? O my lost youth! my cursed and wrecked manhood! If there be a hell blacker than my miserable soul, man has not dreamed of nor language painted it. What would I not give for a fresh, pure, and untrampled heart, such as slumbers peacefully in yonder room, with no damning recollections to scare sleep from her pillow? Innocent childhood!"

His remorse apparently is brief, for he soon fills his goblet with strong wine, lights his cigar, and opens *Candide*.[176]

When sensational incidents are used in these sentimental novels—murders, train or ship wrecks, fires, bodily assaults—the emphasis quickly shifts from the excitement of untoward events to the suffering of characters. A few passages rely upon mystery for suspense, but the domestic sentimentalists do not make great use of the techniques of the adventure novels. They are content to stage most of their action in the quiet circles of representative American homes. The problems in the action of these novels concern duties and decisions, rather than solutions of abnormal events.

Here we have the formula for novels which once sold by the millions of copies, and many best sellers of our day have capitalized upon the same ingredients. Such a mass of Americana as this, softened by sentiment and enriched with cultural allusions, would be instructive even if it had influenced only a small segment of our countrymen, but the additional factor of continuous and widespread popularity of domestic sentimental fiction places books of this *genre* high in the list of our social documents.

Notes

1. In reviewing Mrs. Wilson's last full-length novel, *A Speckled Bird* (Brooklyn *Daily Eagle,* August 23, 1902).

2. A term invented by Carl Van Doren, *The American Novel* (New York: Macmillan Co., 1940), p. 106.

3. Caroline Tichnor, *Hawthorne and His Publisher* (Boston: Houghton Mifflin Co., 1913), p. 141.

4. Basil Hall, *Travels in North America in the Years 1827 and 1828,* 2 vols. (Philadelphia: Carey, Lea & Carey, 1829) II, 261-264.

5. The sources for the early history of Columbus are: (1) John H. Martin, *Columbus, Georgia, from its Selection as a Trading Town in 1827 to its Partial Destruction by Wilson's Raid in 1865* (Columbus, Ga.: Thomas Gilbert, 1874); (2) Nancy Telfair, *A History of Columbus, Georgia: 1828-1928* (Columbus: Historical Pub. Co., 1929); (3) E. Merton Coulter, *A Short History of Georgia* (Chapel Hill: Univ. of No. Carolina Press, 1933); (4) Walter G. Cooper, *The Story of Georgia,* 4 vols, (New York: The American Historical Society, 1938).

6. Information on the early life of Matt Evans has been taken from: (1) the file of Matt Ryan Evans, Department of Archives and History, Montgomery, Alabama; (2) references in Martin, *op. cit.;* (3) family recollections furnished by Mrs. Roy Dallis of LaGrange, Georgia, and by Miss Lily Bragg of Mobile, Alabama.

7. Leonidas Howard, *Sketches of Nehemiah and Edith Howard and Their Descendants* (privately printed, with no reference to place, publisher, or date on the titlepage; the dedication is dated July 4, 1891). A typescript of this genealogy is now in the library of the University of Alabama.

8. The primary sources for dates in this biography are: (1) file of Augusta Evans Wilson, Department of Archives and History, Montgomery, Alabama; (2) file of Matt Ryan Evans, *op. cit.*; (3) family *Bible,* in the possession of Miss Lily Bragg, Mobile; (4) Leonidas Howard, *op. cit.* Miss Lily Bragg is the chief source

for biographical data concerning Mrs. Wilson and her close relatives, for which there is no written record. Miss Mary Gaillard of Mobile, Alabama, a great granddaughter of Lorenzo Madison Wilson, is the chief source for the Wilson family.

9. Sources for the so-called "Creek Wars" are: (1) E. Merton Coulter, *op. cit.*, pp. 212-222; (2) Walter G. Cooper, *op. cit.*, II, 258-285; (3) John H. Martin, *op. cit.*, I, 27-99; (4) Nancy Telfair, *op. cit.*, pp. 40-65.

10. Martin, *op. cit.*, I, 108-129.

11. Information furnished by Mrs. Roy Dallis of LaGrange, Ga.

12. Deed Book A, p. 206, Muscogee County, Georgia, dated March 5, 1839. The date of the foreclosure could not be found by the present Clerk of the Superior Court of Muscogee County. Miss Lily Bragg and Mrs. Roy Dallis are authorities for the information that the foreclosure brought financial ruin to Matt Evans.

13. Mobilienne, "The South's Most Gifted Writer," Mobile *Daily Item*, December 18, 1902, an article based on an interview with Mrs. Wilson.

14. Mary Forrest (Mrs. Julia Deane Freeman), *Women of the South Distinguished in Literature* (New York: Derby & Jackson, 1860), p. 332.

15. Mary Elizabeth Evans was born in Houston on October 16, 1845 (family *Bible* in possession of Miss Lily Bragg).

16. Frederick Law Olmsted, *A Journey Through Texas: or a Saddle-trip on the Southwestern Frontier* (New York: Dix, Edwards & Co., 1857), pp. 55-57.

17. Sources for the information on Texas during the years 1845-1849 are: (1) Olmsted, *op. cit.;* (2) Justin H. Smith, *The War with Mexico,* 2 vols. (New York: Macmillan Co., 1919); (3) Carl Coke Rister, *Border Captives: the Traffic in Prisoners by Southern Plains Indians, 1835-1875* (Norman: University of Oklahoma Press, 1940); (4) J. W. Wilbarger, *Indian Depredations in Texas* (Austin: The Steck Co., 1935); (5) Nathaniel W. Stephenson, *Texas and the Mexican War: a Chronicle of the Winning of the Southwest* (New Haven: Yale University Press, 1921); (6)

William C. Binkley, *The Expansionist Movement in Texas, 1836-1850* (Berkeley: University of California Press, 1925).

18. Augusta J. Evans, *Inez: a Tale of the Alamo* (New York: G. W. Dillingham, 1897), p. 29. The first seven novels by Augusta Evans Wilson—*Inez, Beulah, Macaria, St. Elmo, Vashti, Infelice,* and *At the Mercy of Tiberius*—were issued by Dillingham in a standard edition dated 1887 and 1897, both printings from the same plates. This edition will be used in all quotations and references.

19. Olmsted, *op. cit.*, pp. 151-152.

20. Quoted by Smith, *op. cit.*, I, 103.

21. Mrs. Pickett states, "On Main Street Plaza, near the Alamo, where the First National Bank now stands, was the Evans store, where she, the daughter of the storekeeper, lived" (LaSalle Corbell Pickett, *Literary Hearthstones of Dixie* [Philadephia: J. B. Lippincott, 1912], p. 295).

22. Forrest, *op. cit.*, p. 330.

23. Sources for the information on Mobile during the years 1849-1855 are: (1) Peter J. Hamilton, *Mobile of the Five Flags: the Story of the River Basin and Coast About Mobile from the Earliest Times to the Present* (Mobile: Gill Printing Co., 1913) pp. 247-251; (2) Ervin Craighead, *Mobile: Fact and Tradition* (Mobile: Powers Printing Co., 1930), pp. 188-193; (3) Frederick Law Olmsted, *A Journey in the Seaboard Slave States in the Years 1853-1854 with Remarks on their Economy* (New York: G. P. Putnam's Sons, 1904), pp. 211-225; (4) William H. Milburn, *Ten Years of Preacher-Life* (New York: Derby & Jackson, 1860), pp. 250-315; (5) William H. Milburn, *The Pioneer Preacher: or Rifle, Axe, and Saddle-bags* (New York: Derby & Jackson, 1857), pp. 137-171; (6) files of the Mobile *Advertiser*, Library of Congress; (7) files of the Mobile *Register*, University of Alabama Library.

24. Louis de Vendel Chaudron, *Mobile Mystics and the Story of the Madri-Gras Societies*, Papers of the Iberville Historical Society, No. 2 (the copy in the Library of Congress is stamped "July 11, 1911"), pp. 3-5.

25. Letter from Augusta J. Evans to General P. G. T. Beauregard, dated August 4, 1862, now in the possession of Miss Mary Gaillard of Mobile.

26. The letter is included in an obituary (Mobile *Register,* May 10, 1909, p. 2).

27. *Inez,* p. 242.

28. James Wood Davidson, *The Living Writers of the South* (New York: G. W. Carleton & Co., 1869), p. 622, quoting from the *Southern Quarterly Review.*

29. *Ibid.,* p. 627.

30. Mobilienne, *op. cit.,* Mary Forrest, *op. cit.,* pp. 13-29; J. C. Derby, *Fifty Years Among Authors, Books and Publishers* (New York: G. W. Carleton & Co., 1884), p. 726.

31. Four long letters from Augusta Evans to the Reverend Walter Clopton Harriss are now in the possession of Mrs. R. F. Smith of Oakhill, Alabama. They bear the following dates: January 29, 1856, April 22, 1856, October 12, 1856, and October 29, 1856.

32. *Minutes of the Annual Conferences of the Methodist Episcopal Church South for the Year 1866* (Nashville: Southern Methodist Pub. House, 1870), p. 40.

33. William Fidler, "Unpublished Letters of Henry Timrod," *Southern Literary Messenger,* New Series, II (November, 1940), pp. 605-606. Augusta's answer to Timrod's arguments is contained in a letter to Rachel Lyons, October 17, 1859; the original letter is in the Library of the University of Alabama, a gift of Mrs. W. B. Paterson of Mobile.

34. Copies of two letters by Augusta Evans to Janie Tyler (granddaughter of President John Tyler) dated Jan. 18, 1862, and March 14, 1862, were furnished to the author by Dr. E. P. Lipscomb of Rochester, New York, who obtained copies of them in June, 1885, from a Mrs. Floyd of Richmond, Virginia.

35. Derby, *op. cit.,* p. 391.

36. *The Impending Crisis of the South* is the title of a publication by Hinton Helper, issued in 1857 and adopted as a campaign document by the Republican Party in the election of 1860.

37. "Northern Literature," Mobile *Advertiser,* October 11 and 18, 1859; "Southern Literature," Mobile *Advertiser* October 30, November 6, 1859.

38. Most critics of *St. Elmo, Vashti,* and *Tiberius* have praised or ridiculed Mrs. Wilson's pompous erudition, and these articles contain her characteristic metaphors: "Whose hydra head is a thousand times more self prolific than that of the Lernaean Serpent," and "a monstrous literary *lusus naturae.*" Like her novels, these articles are studded with political, literary, and mythological allusions—all rare and erudite. Numerous references to the periodical literature of the day also point to Miss Evans, whose letters reveal an astonishing knowledge of current magazines. Besides this internal evidence, Miss Evans wrote Rachel Lyons, on January 4, 1860, that she "had to write *two* newspaper articles recently" (photostat of this letter is in the Library of the University of Alabama).

39. General G. H. Thomas, commanding a Federal army in Tennessee (Willis Brewer, *Alabama: Her History, Resources, War Record, and Public Men* [Montgomery: Barrett & Brown], p. 423).

40. Fidler, *op. cit.* The originals of these twenty letters were presented to the Library of the University of Alabama by Mrs. W. B. Paterson of Mobile, a daughter of Rachel Lyons Heustis. The last seven letters in this group were recently edited (William Fidler, "Seven Unpublished Letters by Henry Timrod," *Alabama Review* [April, 1949], II, 139-149). While this biography was in the press, Mrs. Paterson gave the University of Alabama a valuable copy of the 1860 edition of Timrod's *Poems* (Boston: Ticknor and Fields), containing the poet's autograph and a graceful presentation poem, "To R. L.," also in the poet's handwriting.

41. Derby, *op. cit.,* pp. 391-393.

42. New York *World,* June 20, 1860.

43. The house was given the name of "Georgia Cottage" by its builder, Mrs. Mary del Barco Hardaway, who used slave labor from Georgia in its construction. Augusta purchased the place in 1860 and registered the deed in her father's name.

44. May 29, 1860. A photostat of this letter and of seventeen

others to Rachel Lyons (dated October 17 and December 8, 1859; January 4, July 30, August 28, and November 15, 1860; February 2, August 20, and October 3, 1861; January 22, May 31, and September 24, 1862; March 20, June 14, September 12, and November 21, 1863; and May 1, 1864) are on file in the Library of the University of Alabama; the originals of six of these letters were presented to the University of Alabama by Mrs. W. B. Paterson of Mobile, a daughter of Rachel Lyons Heustis. Two letters to Rachel Lyons, dated January 21, 1860, and June 26, 1861, are in the possession of Mrs. Rosalie Heustis Clark of Birmingham. Copies were furnished by Mr. J. E. Rice, WPA Historical Records Survey.

45. *Ibid.,* January 21, 1860. Her references are slightly inaccurate: Comte died in 1857 and Hamilton in 1856.

46. July 30, 1860. Six additional letters by Augusta to Rachel Lyons (dated February 16, 1860; March 28 [1863]; February 28 and March 18, 1864; July 23 [ca. 1895]; and August 8, [1896]) are in the Library of the University of Alabama, to which they were presented by Miss Mabel Heustis of Mobile, a daughter of Rachel Lyons Heustis.

47. *Ibid.,* March 28, [1863].

48. "Prospectus" of the New *World,* June 9, 1860.

49. *DeBow's Review* (October, 1859), XVII, 491.

50. "Beulah," *Methodist Quarterly Review* (January, 1860), XX, 112.

51. A publisher's advertisement of *Beulah,* New York *World,* June 14, 1860.

52. *The Southern Literary Messenger* (October, 1860), XXXI, 248.

53. Derby, *op. cit.,* pp. 390-391.

54. *Ibid.,* p. 392.

55. Letter by Augusta J. Evans to Mrs. L. Virginia French, January 13, 1861, original now in the possession of Mrs. Fred Frazier of Chattanooga; a copy was furnished by Miss Virginia Peck of Troy, Alabama.

56. Letter to Janie Tyler, March 14, 1862, *op. cit.*

57. *Ibid.*

58. *Appleton's Cyclopedia of American Biography.*

59. "Correspondence of Thomas Reade Rootes Cobb, 1860-1862," *Publications of the Southern History Association* (July, 1907), XI, 241.

60. *Ibid.*, p. 245.

61. *Dictionary of American Biography*, IX, 54-5.

62. Thomas Cooper DeLeon, "Biographical Reminiscences," *Devota* (New York: G. W. Dillingham Co., 1913), pp. 151-155; Mobile *Advertiser*, March 20, 1926.

63. Letter to Janie Tyler, January 18, 1862, *op. cit.*

64. Augusta J. Evans to General P. G. T. Beauregard, August 4, 1862, original now in the possession of Miss Mary Gaillard of Mobile, Alabama.

65. Letter to Janie Tyler, March 14, 1862, *op. cit.*

66. Letter to Janie Tyler, January 18, 1862, *op. cit.*

67. Eleven letters by Augusta Evans to Jabez Lamar Monroe Curry are on file among the Curry Papers, Division of Manuscripts, Library of Congress; microfilm copies are in the Library of the University of Alabama. The dates of these letters are: November 10, 1862, December 20, 1862, July 15, 1863, October 16, 1863, January 27, 1864, October 7, 1865, April 15, 1866, May 7, 1866, June 22, 1866, January 9, 1867, and January 1, 1902. All references to her letters to Curry refer to this collection.

68. Letter to General P. G. T. Beauregard, August 4, 1862, *op. cit.*

69. A clipping of the article, with the author's autograph, is on file in the Curry Papers, Library of Congress, *op. cit.*

70. Original in possession of Mrs. Rosalie Heustis Clark of Birmingham, Alabama.

71. LaSalle Corbell Pickett, *op. cit.*, pp. 289-290.

72. James Ryder Randall, *Maryland My Maryland and Other Poems* (Baltimore: John Murphy Co., 1908), pp. 12, 16.

73. *Ibid.*, p. 66.

74. Letter to Rachel Lyons, February 8, 1864, original in the Library of the University of Alabama.

75. Letter to Rachel Lyons, March 18, 1864, original in the Library of the University of Alabama.

76. Letters to Rachel Lyons, originals in the Library of the University of Alabama.

77. Letter by General P. G. T. Beauregard to Augusta J. Evans, March 24, 1863, original in the Louisiana Historical Association, New Orleans, Louisiana.

78. Mrs. E. S. Sledge of Mobile owned a copy of the Confederate edition in 1940. Mrs. Sledge is the present owner of "Georgia Cottage."

79. Derby, *op. cit.*, pp. 392-394.

80. A. B. Moore, *History of Alabama and Her People*, 3 vols. (Chicago: American Historical Society, 1927), I, 557.

81. Brewer, *op. cit.*, p. 423.

82. "Without household manufacture, the war would not have lasted long" (Moore, *op. cit.*, I, 554).

83. Louise Manly, "Augusta Evans Wilson: 1835-1909," *Library of Southern Literature*, edited by E. A. Alderman and J. C. Harris (Atlanta: Martin & Hoyt, 1910), XIII, 5842; Francis Arant, "St. Elmo Recalled," Birmingham *News*, April 3, 1927.

84. *Macaria*, chapter xxx.

85. Letter by General Beauregard to Augusta J. Evans, *op. cit.*

86. Chapters xxvii-xxviii, *passim.*

87. *Ibid.*

88. Chapters xx-xxi, *passim.*

89. Letter to Curry, October 16, 1863, *op. cit.*

90. Letter to Curry, January 27, 1864, *op. cit.*

91. Chapters xxxii-xxxvi, *passim.*

92. Letter to Curry, December 20, 1862, *op. cit.*

93. Letter to Curry, July 15, 1863, *op. cit.*

94. Letter to Curry, January 27, 1864, *op. cit.*

95. Haywood J. Pearce, *Benjamin H. Hill: Secession and Reconstruction* (Chicago: University of Chicago Press, 1928), p. 107.

96. Letter to Curry, October 7, 1865, *op. cit.*

97. Pleasant A. Stovall, *Robert Toombs: Statesman, Speaker, Soldier, Sage* (New York: Cassell Pub. Co., 1892), p. 302.

98. Frances Arant, *op. cit.*

99. Derby, *op. cit.*, p. 393.

100. Letter to Curry, October 7, 1865, *op. cit.*

101. Derby, *op. cit.*, p. 395.

102. Letter to Curry, October 7, 1865, *op. cit.*

103. Letter to Curry, June 22, 1866, *op. cit.*

104. Arthur B. Maurice, "Best Sellers of Yesterday: I—Augusta Jane Evans's *St. Elmo*," *Bookman* (March, 1910), XXXI, 35.

105. New York Daily *Tribune*, December 13, 1866.

106. *Ibid.*, January 12, 1867.

107. *Ibid.*, March 28, 1867.

108. Hamilton W. Mabie, "The Most Popular Novels in America," *Forum* (December, 1893), XVI, 509.

109. Montrose J. Moses, *The Literature of the South* (New York: Thomas Y. Crowell, 1910), p. 331.

110. Fred Lewis Pattee, *The Feminine Fifties* (New York: Appleton-Century Co., 1940), p. 125.

111. *St. Elmo*, p. 314.

112. A review of *St. Elmo*, New York *Times*, January 5, 1867.

113. *Ibid.*

114. Letter to the Reverend Walter Harriss, October 12, 1856, *op. cit.*

115. Letter to Curry, January 9, 1867, *op. cit.*

116. Thomas Cooper DeLeon, "Augusta Evans Wilson," St. Louis *Globe Democrat*, January 9, 1898.

117. [Arthur B. Maurice], "*St. Elmo* and Its Author," *Bookman* (September, 1902), XVI, 12.

118. Maurice, "Best Sellers of Yesterday," *op. cit.*, p. 42.

119. DeLeon, "Biographical Reminiscences," *op. cit.*, p. 174.

120. Mobile *Register*, May 10, 1909, p. 2. This article, one of several obituaries in the *Register*, was written by someone who knew Mrs. Wilson very well.

121. Letter to Curry, October 7, 1865, *op. cit.*

122. Charles H. Webb, *St. Twel'mo: or the Cuneiform Cyclopedist of Chattanooga* (New York: C. H. Webb Publisher, 1867), p. 7. Copies of *St. Twel'mo* are available in the Library of Con-

gress and in the Mobile Public Library. Webb also wrote *Liffith Lank: or Lunacy* (1866), a parody of Charles Reade's *Griffith Gaunt;* another work by Webb is the witty satire *The Wickedest Woman in New York* (1868).

123. *St. Elmo,* pp. 154-155. This passage is amusingly satirized in *St. Twel'mo,* pp. 43-44.

124. *St. Elmo,* pp. 107-108.

125. *St. Elmo,* p. 395. The battle against the feminist movement is waged similarly in the following passages of Mrs. Wilson's works: *Macaria,* p. 122; *Infelice,* pp. 128-130; *A Speckled Bird,* pp. 76, 119-121, 167-168.

126. Mobile *Register,* "Sixty Years Ago," December 19, 1948.

127. Files on the Chicago Theatre, by courtesy of Professor Napier Wilt, University of Chicago; also, advertisments and notices in the New York *Times* and the Brooklyn *Daily Eagle* for the years 1909-1912.

128. New York *Dramatic Mirror,* (December 25, 1909), LXII, 5.

129. Letter by Joseph H. Moskowitz of Twentieth Century-Fox Corporation to the author, January 8, 1947.

130. John Shirley Ward, a review of *St. Elmo, Scott's Monthly Magazine,* (March, 1867), III, 222.

131. Letter to Curry, October 7, 1865, *op. cit.*

132. Letter to Curry, June 22, 1866, *op. cit.*

133. Letter to Curry, May 7, 1866, *op. cit.*

134. File of Curry Papers, *op. cit.*

135. Atlanta *Journal,* May 10, 1909.

136. A recollection of Mrs. Madison Gaillard, furnished by her daughter, Miss Mary Gaillard.

137. Davidson, *op. cit.,* p. 628.

138. Accounts of this incident were furnished by Miss Lily Bragg and Miss Mary Gaillard; DeLeon, "Biographical Reminiscences," *op. cit.,* p. 163, gives a brief description of it.

139. Contributed by Miss Lily Bragg.

140. "Mrs. Wilson in War Times," Mobile *Register,* May 10, 1909.

141. Reprint of a Louisville *Courier-Journal* article, undated but either November or December, 1887, in possession of Dr. Burke Johnston of Virginia Polytechnic Institute.

142. DeLeon, St. Louis *Globe Democrat, op. cit.*

143. Reprinted in the Talladega (Ala.) *Watchtower*, December 8, 1869.

144. Davidson, *op. cit.*, p. 627.

145. Montgomery *Advertiser*, November 26, 1887.

146. DeLeon, St. Louis *Globe Democrat, op. cit.*

147. Mobile *Register*, July 15, 1871.

148. DeLeon, "Biographical Reminiscences," *op. cit.*, pp. 171-173.

149. Sources for this passage are: (1) Montgomery *Daily Advertiser*, March 24, 1883, reprinted from the Chicago *Tribune;* (2) Montgomery *Daily Advertiser*, February 22, 1885, reprinted from the New York *Sun;* (3) Derby, *op. cit.*, p. 398, quoting from an article which appeared in the Louisville *Courier-Journal;* (4) undated article (probably December, 1887) which is reprinted from the Louisville *Courier-Journal*, in possession of Dr. Burke Johnston of Blacksburg, Va.; (5) DeLeon, St. Louis *Globe Democrat, op. cit.*

150. Contributed by Miss Lily Bragg.

151. Contributed by Miss Mary Gaillard.

152. Contributed by Miss Lily Bragg, who was informed of the English movie by a friend who saw it in England.

153. Letter to Mr. N. Harris, U. S. Consul at Leeds, File of Augusta Evans Wilson, Alabama Collection, Library of the University of Alabama.

154. Birmingham *News*, December 31, 1939; Tuscaloosa *News*, January 8, 1940; Mildred B. Mitcham, "A Tale in the Making: the Face in the Window," *Southern Folklore Quarterly*, (December, 1948), XII, 241-257.

155. Contributed by Dr. Edward H. Cary, Dallas, Texas.

156. Anon., "Photosensitive Glass Developed by Corning," *Chemical and Engineering News* (June 23, 1947), XXV, 1822;

Karlem Riess, *etals.*, "Photosensitive Glass," *American Journal of Physics* (October, 1948), XVI, 399-403.

157. Letter to the author, January 5, 1940.

158. Ethel Hodgson, "Augusta Evans Wilson," Montgomery *Advertiser*, December 17, 1905.

159. Files on the Chicago Theatre, courtesy of Professor Napier Wilt, *op. cit.*

160. Contributed by Miss Lily Bragg.

161. The article which Professor Wyman appears to answer is that of November 26, 1887. Though unsigned, Professor Wyman's article, Tuscaloosa *Gazette*, December 8, 1887, was attributed to him by Mrs. Wilson (see following note).

162. Letter to Professor W. S. Wyman, December 12, [1887], the original in the possession of Miss Alice Wyman of Tuscaloosa, Alabama.

163. New York *Daily Tribune*, November 18, 1887.

164. DeLeon, St. Louis *Globe Democrat*, *op. cit.*

165. *Ibid.*

166. DeLeon, "Biographical Reminiscences," *op. cit.*, pp. 130-131.

167. *Ibid.*, p. 195.

168. Mobilienne, *op. cit.*

169. Brooklyn *Daily Eagle*, August 23, 1902.

170. "A Fable by Mrs. Wilson," *Bookman* (November, 1902), XVI, 230-232.

171. Louisville *Post*, August 2, 1902.

172. In January, 1950, the surviving close relatives of Mrs. Wilson are: two nieces, Miss Lily Bragg of Mobile, and Mrs. Alma Tarleton Norris of Washington, D. C.; two nephews, Mr. Clarence Vivian Evans of Mobile, and Mr. John Bragg of Los Angeles, California.

173. Caroline Tichnor, *op. cit.*, p. 141.

174. Herbert Ross Brown, *The Sentimental Novel in America: 1789-1860* (Durham: Duke Univ. Press, 1940), p. 322.

175. *Vashti*, pp. 42-43.

176. *St. Elmo*, p. 81.

Index